RELIGIOUS LIFE
IN AMERICA

RELIGIOUS LIFE
IN AMERICA

A RECORD OF PERSONAL OBSERVATION

BY

ERNEST HAMLIN ABBOTT

NEW YORK
THE OUTLOOK COMPANY
1902

THE DEVINNE PRESS

TO MY FATHER

CONTENTS

vii

PREFACE

IN the year 1901, at the request of The Outlook, I undertook a journey through parts of the United States for the purpose of making, and recording in a series of articles, observations of religious life in America. This book is the record of that journey. It is not a study in methods of church activity. Nor is it a record of scientific investigation. All possibility of any result at all scientific was at once eliminated by these two conditions of the trip — on the one hand, the field traversed, covering eighteen States of the Union scattered through a territory bounded by Canada, the Atlantic Ocean, the Gulf of Mexico, and the Rocky Mountains; on the other hand, the time, scarcely more than three months. Neither is this book an essay on the deeper spiritual life of the American people. That there is such deeper spiritual life may, I think, be fairly inferred from the facts here recorded, and its nature may in some degree be at least surmised; but it would be presumption to suppose that in three months that could be discovered in a nation by a traveler which in an individual may be hidden for years from the closest friend. Besides, it will be readily understood by readers that it is generally the most significant personal experiences which are not subject for public discussion. We must, then, be content, my readers and I, with certain deliberately accepted limitations: we must not expect to find anything which lies much below the surface, and we must not count on establishing any great conclusion by scientific method. Whatever value this book will have must consist in the fact that it is a record of occurrences pertaining to religion in America in the first year of the twentieth century as they were observed by one traveler — as indeed they might have been observed by any one of ordinary learning and discernment.

To the Rev. F. S. Spalding, rector of St. Paul's Church, Erie, Pennsylvania, I am glad to express my obligation for the idea which suggested this journey of observation. Also to the many who, by cordial hospitality, generous offer of time, frank and unreserved expressions of opinion and statements of fact, by coöperation indeed in many ways, made it easy for me to carry out the plan of the journey, I renew my thanks. Not least to the known and unknown correspondents and critics who, by letters, editorial comments, and in some cases speeches, have supplied information on the subjects described and discussed in my articles, I acknowledge my indebtedness. This information has been of value to me in revising the articles for their publication in the present form. Words of commendation and corroboration have in a few instances led me to change statements from a tentative to an unqualified form. Certain corrections have enabled me to make changes in the direction of accuracy. And adverse criticisms, some vehement, many in good spirit, and a few delightfully brisk of wit, have indicated a number of passages where the meaning evidently was not perfectly clear or the phraseology infelicitous. I have availed myself of these criticisms in modifying or amplifying some statements, so that they will be, I think, more intelligible.

Now I invite my readers to set out upon that road over which I have journeyed. I hope they may have on the way some of the same enjoyment and gain some of the same profit that I received as I traveled over it.

E. H. A.

CORNWALL-ON-HUDSON,
October, 1902.

THE WORKINGMAN AND
THE CHURCH

I

THE WORKINGMAN AND
THE CHURCH

WHEN I reached Baltimore, four facts were especially associated in my mind with that city: that it is the center of Roman Catholicism in America; that it is the seat of Johns Hopkins University; that it is famous for the beauty and *mise élégante* of its women; and that it is to terrapin and wild duck what Paris is said to be to Americans — the place to which they are sure to go if they are good. It was, therefore, one of the last places to which I should have chosen to go in order to study industrial problems.

I did stop at Baltimore for the purpose of getting some information from the authorities of the Roman Catholic Church and incidentally of seeing the President of the University; as

3

a matter of fact, I remained several days because of the acquaintance I made with workingmen of the city. Most unexpectedly, my visit to Baltimore resulted in my getting one of the points of view of the organized laborers for which I had no such chance in any other place.

The General Secretary of the Baltimore Young Men's Christian Association put me in the way of meeting a number of men connected with the labor unions of Baltimore. This fact did not occasion in me such surprise as it would have if it had occurred later in my trip, for generally I found the secretaries of these Associations out of touch (though I believe not out of sympathy) with the workingmen. Here, however, as in one or two other places, I found an exception — a man of evident good breeding, strong personality, businesslike ways, broad sympathies, alert mind — the kind of true gentleman we Americans are proud to think only a democracy can produce. It was merely by chance that I happened to go to the Association, and, when I had met the Secretary, again it was merely by chance that in conversation I inquired about the relation of the workingmen of Baltimore to the Association. He confessed that there were but few workingmen among the members. Naturally, not many men who worked all day with their hands would be likely to care for exercise in the gymnasium. A few every year took advantage of the evening classes. Almost none were engaged in the distinctively religious work of the Association. This was a matter of concern to him. That it was due to indifference on his part was contradicted by his whole spirit. The very fact that our conversation naturally turned to the subject of the religious feeling of the workingman was sufficient proof of that. There seemed to be a chasm between the Association and the workingman which no devising on his part had yet succeeded in bridging. How natural it was for the workingmen to be found on the one side of this chasm and the Association on the other was brought out by what this Secretary told me of a political controversy then still unsettled.

There was in Baltimore a rather strict Sunday law. It forbade almost all sales on Sunday; it not only prohibited the sale of liquor, but also of cigars, soda-water, and newspapers at the small shops. For some time that part of the law pertaining to the small shops had remained unenforced. Then began a movement for gen-

eral enforcement of law — one of those spasms
of public virtue characteristic of America — and
these small shops were shut up. Thereupon
came this curious division of public sentiment.
On the one side were the labor unions and what
is called the plain people, who desired that that
part of the law which pertained to the small
shops should be repealed. On the other side
were the churches and the ministers and the
Young Men's Christian Association, who desired to maintain the law on the statute-books
unchanged. Here was an issue distinctly joined
between what we may call the religious party
and the unreligious party. The significance of
the issue is in the motives which lay behind the
two positions. The religious party did not have
any animosity toward the small shops — in fact,
they were not by any means united that the
shops should be closed; but they were concerned
in the preservation of an institution — the Puritan Sabbath — and feared the weakening of the
law that maintained that institution, preferring
to leave the law as it was, partly unenforced,
than to endanger the whole law by the repeal of
any portion. This was the position of the Secretary as he stated it to me. The other party
were in opposition to these religious people, not

because they did not care for a quiet, uncommercial Sunday, but because they cared more for what they believed to be the welfare of the small shopkeepers, who needed all the custom they could get. Behind one party was the power of the strong public opinion which in America traditionally supports Sunday observance. Behind the other was that more nearly universal power of men's direct interest in the concerns of their neighbors. It is a mistake to think that ethical considerations in every conflict of this sort are all on one side. Certainly in this instance there was some moral earnestness on each side; only on one side it was the conscious moral earnestness of men not altogether enlightened fighting to preserve an institution, while on the other side it was the unconscious — but therefore perhaps the more praiseworthy — moral earnestness of men not altogether enlightened either, but imbued with strong personal human sympathy.

Aroused as I was by the conversation I had with the Secretary of the Young Men's Christian Association, I was glad to accept his suggestion that he should put me in the way of meeting some of the leaders among the workingmen. For this purpose he introduced me

to a Methodist minister whom he knew to be
acquainted with members of the trades unions.

It was Monday morning, the time for ministers' meetings. We went together to the gathering-place of the Methodists. It was in a
small hall over a book-store. As we went up
the stairs I heard the sound of loud voices engaged in what seemed to be rather violent
discussion. As I waited in the anteroom for
the Secretary to find the minister we came to
see, I could hear a man vigorously making
some sort of self-defense. He was frequently
interrupted by others in contradiction. When
the minister whom we had come to see appeared, he at once apologized for the heat of
the discussion in which his "brethren" were
engaged.

It transpired that the controversy was about
a matter of "transfers." Some of the more
"desirable" churches of the city — that is,
churches paying the highest salaries and containing the most influential people socially —
had been filled by men from outside the city.
Against this injustice, as they apparently
counted it, some of the ministers of less "desirable" churches were protesting; they believed
that they themselves ought to have these more

" desirable " places before outsiders. The altercation in the hall became so noisy, and its character so distracting, that we found it difficult to carry on any conversation in the anteroom. I have been assured that such an incident ought not to be considered as of common occurrence; and that, moreover, in the eyes of those who value the Methodist polity as an essential in efficient Christian activity, it looked like a fight for principle. To the workingman, however, whose interest in machinery does not extend to the ecclesiastical variety, it is not easy to explain that there is a moral distinction between a struggle by ministers for higher salaries and a struggle by workingmen for higher wages. One " outsider," at any rate, thought he found in the controversy at the Monday meeting some light on that chasm between the workingman and the churches.

In less boisterous surroundings I had a brief conversation with this minister whose distinction was that he actually was well acquainted with some members of the labor unions and understood their point of view. He was perfectly candid in his opinion that the chief reason for the alienation of most workingmen from the churches was the fact that, as a rule,

ministers were not in sympathy with the under
dog. He instanced a great strike there in Baltimore on the trolley lines. In his opinion the
men had a grievance. The question of putting
vestibules on the cars was involved. The company brought a number of its employees into
the council-chamber where an investigation
was being carried on; and when the question
was put to them, their hands, bleeding from
exposure, went up — against the vestibules.
"A most flagrant piece of intimidation!" he
exclaimed. In spite of such incidents as this,
he said, there were only two other ministers
besides himself who publicly spoke of it — one
of whom was Dr. Babcock, honored there, as
later in New York, for his virility and human
feeling. The subject was brought up at the
conference, whereupon a "brother" (*sic*)
brushed it aside by saying, "It is our business
simply to preach the Gospel." The unions
felt, justly or unjustly, that the churches didn't
care. In brief, as he put it, he believed the
churches of all denominations were "weak
between Sundays."

I must confess this account of ministerial
professionalism intensified my dislike of the
cant term "brother." It made me wonder

whether the workingmen would not be justified in asking for a living parable in answer to the question, " Who is my ' brother ' ? " Is it the man who on his way to preach the Gospel passes by on the other side? In a later chapter I shall relate an experience of mine which shows that in some places in America this answering parable is being embodied in real life.

What the Methodist minister told me of the workingman's feelings was confirmed in an interview he enabled me to have with a former President of the Baltimore Federation of Labor. I was surprised to find that a leader in this movement should seem to be so young a man. He left his work on a linotype machine in the middle of the afternoon to have a talk with me. At first he was very cautious in what he said, for he suspected from a remark I made that I was on a political errand in behalf of Sunday legislation; but as soon as I cleared that up he was very candid.

" Religion is in a bad way in Baltimore," he said, with the air of a man who has bad news to tell and has given up the attempt to break it gently. " I say frankly that the churches do not welcome the workingmen, and the workingmen do not care for the churches. The churches are made up mostly of employers, and they are trying to get all they can out of their men, and don't care for them as men at all."

"Granted all that," said I, passing by without comment the very obvious exaggeration, "suppose that the churches really should want to do something for the workingmen, what would you suggest?"

"Why," he replied, quite as eager to propose a positive plan as he was vehement in his censure — "why don't they give lectures on industrial questions on Sunday? Why don't ministers send out circulars to the leaders of the various unions saying something like this: 'Next Sunday I am going to give a talk on arbitration, and am going to have a number of the most influential capitalists present in the congregation, and I want every union in the city represented there also. I do not intend to take sides one way or the other.'"

"Would such a proposition be welcomed by the unions?"

"I think decidedly it would. But then the ministers in this city would never do such a thing. When there is any strike or labor difficulty before the public, you do not hear of any sermons about it; the ministers are afraid to express an opinion, for those churches are under the control of the employing classes. You hear sermons about everything else, but you don't hear any sermons about the workingman."

" I suppose workingmen would expect sermons to uphold Socialism? "

" I don't believe in any 'ism,' " was his prompt reply. " I try to be liberal." His conception of Socialism I inferred from his adding: " There are a lot of Polish Hebrews in Baltimore who are Debs men, but they are about all there is to the Social Democracy."

As to ministers he was as explicit as he was with regard to churches:

" They go where they get the most salaries. If they can get two hundred dollars more, they go there."

After my experience at the ministers' meeting I was not in the mood to deny that; but I asked: " Is that not true of workingmen as well? Does not the workingman go where he gets more wages? Why shouldn't the minister have the same right?"

" I don't blame any man," he replied, " for

getting all he can; but when he does it, I want him not to pretend to go for some other reason; for I call that getting money under false pretenses."

When in the course of our conversation we reverted to the Sunday law, he represented the workingman as considering it an interference with his rightful mode of recreation.

"To the workingman Sunday is the day when he has a chance to get rest and recreation, particularly Sunday afternoon, when he goes with his family to some of these resorts and spends the afternoon there. By the way, why don't the ministers go to the resorts themselves? The workingmen are down there, and there isn't one who wouldn't be glad to have a minister come down and hold service and preach. Workingmen all believe in God and justice, but they want sympathy, and feel that they don't get it from the ministers. Another thing the ministers can do is to get a list of the labor unions, and then request the secretary of each union for permission to attend the union meeting, and the union would be glad to have him come and address them and preach on any matter—only not about heaven."

"What, in your opinion, is the Young Men's

Christian Association worth to workingmen?"
was another question I asked.

"Well," he replied, "it costs six dollars a
year to belong, and there's not much charity
in that."

"But do the workingmen want charity?"

"Not a bit of it!" was his quick rejoinder.
For a moment, however, he seemed nonplussed.
Then he added, as if he wished to remove
any impression of antagonism he may have un-
intentionally made: "You could really educate
the workingmen up to recognizing the advantages that such an organization as the Young
Men's Christian Association does offer. After
all, you cannot do anything unless you tackle
the young boys. And let me tell you," he continued, in the most deliberative strain, "that is
the strength of the Catholic Church; they get
hold of the children, and then put into their
ignorant heads the idea that they must contribute to the Church so much for St. Peter's pence
and so much for other things; and then they
scrape and starve and even steal to do it; and
they teach them also that they must confess
and so on, and as a consequence when they
grow up they are in the Church. You've got
to get hold of the young boys. Now, I've got

two young boys, and I've made them join the Young Men's Christian Association."

The opinions expressed by this labor leader may, I think, be considered fairly representative of the ordinary labor union member's views on the institutions of Christianity. For three reasons. First, there was nothing very original about them. They came to be familiar to me by repetition in conversations I had with others. Second, this man, as I ascertained later, was ambitious to be a political leader among workingmen, and as he knew he was "talking for publication" (and, by the way, was rather pleased to do so), it may safely be assumed that he was discreet in his account of what workingmen thought. Third, in comparing him with the other labor leaders of the city whom I met at a meeting of the Federation of Labor, I should say that both by temperament and by training he was best qualified to state their case with a minimum of intrusive "personal equation." In reporting his views, I do not venture to pass any judgment upon their accuracy. So far as they are based upon fact, they call attention to conditions which it is the function of the Church to change. So far as they are based upon ignorance of the real attitude of the Church, they call attention to misapprehensions which it is the function of the Church to remove. Misapprehensions are quite as potent in alienating men from one another as outward conditions can be.

At the meeting of the Federation of Labor, to which I have just referred, I was most cordially welcomed. Upon the request of several labor leaders and sympathizers, I was persuaded, rather against my own instincts, to put some questions from the floor. While I waited my turn I was given a seat on the platform. The meeting was characterized by what seemed to me acerbity of feeling, not only in regard to capitalists, but in one instance in regard to one of the federated labor unions. Although it was an open meeting for the transaction of routine business, I felt as if I were at a council of war. After I had put my questions, all pertaining to the workingman and the Church, a delegate rose and, with great dignity and courtesy, called the attention of the delegates to the fact that it was contrary to the constitution to discuss any political or sectarian question at a meeting of the Federation. I hastened to remove, if possible, the impression of sectarianism which the wording of one of my questions had unfortunately created. A number of the delegates argued in favor of a discussion of the questions; but the decision was adverse to a discussion. The incident, however, was by no means fruitless. It was noteworthy for two things: first, the disappearance of all sign of acrimony during the presentation and discussion of the questions about religion; second, the unmistakable and almost eager interest which the delegates evinced throughout.

After the meeting a number of the men came up and made some further inquiries about my questions. I made special acquaintance with one of these who had been foremost in attempting to have my questions discussed. I had noticed his face and mien as being exceptional for his surroundings. This was partly due, as I discovered, to the nature of his trade, the finer part of photolithography. He accompanied me on my way from the hall to the hotel where I had a room. He was greatly interested in the object of my trip, and especially in its bearing on the religion of workingmen. He was inclined to be disheartened concerning industrial conditions, but his discontent was not that of a pessimist, but rather that of an idealist. He told me much about himself, and as he talked his idealism showed itself not only in language but also in a quiet emphasis of look and gesture.

He had been brought up a Roman Catholic. He had found himself, however, remonstrating against the emphasis which that Church laid on patient endurance of wrong. This was contrary to all his instincts as an American workingman. As a workingman he was conscious of unjust social conditions; as an American he was conscious of his right to struggle against them. He could not believe a man could cure injustice by patiently enduring it. He therefore not only broke away from the Church, but arrayed himself against it as the chief power which paralyzed men's efforts for an ideal social order. He felt, too, the inadequacy and even the perverseness of labor unions as a force for social improvement. "A few years ago," he said, " I was active in the Federation of Labor; but now, though I am a delegate, I cannot work in the organization with any enthusiasm. It seems as if workingmen were bound to injure themselves by their own actions. They are blindly selfish and bitter and shortsighted in their organized procedure. They have no proper, suitable, and intelligent lead-

ers. This is due to conditions under which
they work. They have no chance to educate
themselves or to train leaders from their own
ranks. Now, in an ideal state of society that
would not be possible." This brought him to
an enthusiastic statement of his belief in the
Single Tax. Henry George was his prophet,
and Henry George's idealistic political economy
was his theology. He had reacted from the
materialism which he saw apparently govern-
ing the workingmen with whom he was associated. In place of it he had this conviction,
which, more than anything else he said, may
be called his creed: "I believe that mind con-
trols matter."

When I asked him for his judgment of the
saloon, his idealism was very evident in his answer: "Saloons do harm to the workingmen.
They not only create intemperance, but injure
men who are temperate. For instance, most of
the labor unions meet in halls that are provided
by saloon-keepers, who charge nothing for their
use. After a labor union meeting is over, all
the men go down to the saloon and conscien-
tiously remain there and pay for drinks in order
to remunerate their benefactor. A great many
men who would otherwise not drink at all be-

come intemperate through this conscientious attempt to repay obligations."

The fact that a meeting-place was provided for the unions was a good thing? Yes, he was sure of that. The social element involved helped to further comradeship and harmony? Yes. Was there anything to take the place of the saloon in this service to organized labor? No, there was not, and he did not see how there could be. Could a church make provision for a hall and good-fellowship? No, he thought that would be savoring too much of charity — it would come from the outside; it would be unnatural. "Since, then, this is a necessary service," I inquired, "and the saloon is doing it, and you can imagine no efficient substitute, is not the saloon a benefit to the workingman, after all?"

"Well," was his answer, "it *is* practically, but not *ideally*. Perhaps I think too much of ideal states of society. When I speak of a thing as right or wrong, I think of it as it ought to be, not as it is."

Though politically ambitious and in a small way successful, he had put his idealism into his politics. Though a Democrat and a believer in Bryan, he refused a nomination that was tendered to him because its acceptance would involve his being expected to vote for Gorman, in whom he had no confidence.

Strangely, the idealism which he applied so invariably to his moral conceptions and to his politics he had never apparently attempted to apply to religion. In his mind was so firmly embedded his youthful conception that religion was a visible wafer, a smell of incense, an audible confession, a life of submission to materialism, that it seems never to have occurred to him that religion might be of the same nature with his many ideals, much less that it should be their very flower. It seemed a sad commentary on the inefficiency of at least one branch of the Church of Jesus Christ in this twentieth century that a mind trained in that branch of the Church, and possessed of native qualities that at times seemed such as are produced only by the long process of academic education, should, in spite of its inborn idealism, be capable of entertaining such a conception of religion as this:

"If by religion you mean that which is divine, I don't believe there is any such thing. I don't believe there is any divinity. I believe that religion originated somewhat in this way: A number of years ago there was a man [meaning Jesus] who preached social reforms; and he was so far ahead of his time that his followers attributed to him something divine [referring to the magic of the mass], and that is the way religion began."

Before we separated I think both of us got a better conception of the religion of Jesus than we had before; for we found it grounded in the universal sense of moral obligation and the universal honor paid to self-sacrifice for others. The rest of our conversation was of the sort that all men instinctively consider confidential. Indeed, though I shall not be likely ever to forget its impression, its form I did not attempt in any way to preserve. It will be enough to say that it revealed a mind whose idealism, untrained as it was, seemed to me as much truer and deeper than the transcendental philosophy of Emerson as it was marked by a clearer, more unstudied, more sincere unselfishness.

THE CHURCH AND THE
WORKINGMAN

II

THE CHURCH AND THE
WORKINGMAN

PROBABLY the attention which I shall give to the industrial problem will seem to most readers to be disproportionate to other phases of religious life in America. Certainly the intimate connection between religious life and social problems in America was a surprise to me; indeed, when I finished my trip, I had the feeling that I had failed in my purpose, and that I had been observing phenomena, not of religion, but of sociology. If any generalization is justifiable from such evidence as I have gathered, it is that religion in America is characterized not so much by devoutness as by righteousness, less by the look upward than by the look outward.

Carlyle divided the people of Great Britain

into two sects, the Dandiacal Body and the Drudges. My observation has led me to believe that this classification can be said to be measurably true of America as well. "To the psychological eye," Carlyle said, "these sects reveal not only their secular significance, but their religious character as well." In America, too, this separation between the "leisure class" and the "working people" has its religious bearing plain to those who look for it. Perhaps the dwellers in Baltimore are too near the subject to avoid strabismus in looking at these two sects in their own city, or to avoid myopy in looking at them as they exist elsewhere. There were three men of the city, however, whom I met that seemed to have pretty straight and clear vision.

One of these was the pastor of a Methodist church in the poorer quarter of the city. His experiences among working people in England as well as in America were wider and more intimate than those of any other minister I have had occasion to meet. With the possible exception of an Episcopalian clergyman in Augusta, Georgia, and a Presbyterian clergyman in St. Louis, no man in active ministerial work, among all those whom I met during my travels, was living as nearly exclusively among wage-earners as he.

"The peculiarity of the workingmen of Baltimore," he said to me, "is that their whole mind is directed on food, clothes, and a good time. What is true of the workingman in this respect is true of the whole city of Baltimore. In Boston, it is said, they ask, 'How much do you know?' in New York, 'How much are you worth?' in Philadelphia, 'Who's your father?' and in Baltimore, 'What is there to eat?' This materialism in all conditions of life is the worst enemy of the churches. Among workingmen it results not so much in hostility as in indifference. When men are mainly set upon supplying their physical wants, it is not strange that the churches, which in this city are mainly concerned not with this life but with the future life, should have no appeal for them. It is the religiosity and the lack of sincerity in the churches that repel the workingmen. As a consequence they go to resorts for sensations. As to the very poor men — and it is among these that I work — they haven't the clothes they think they should wear at church; besides, they are tired after work. The commercial spirit is driving the working world. In this respect England

differs from America; there the close organization of the unions enables the workingmen to
work more slowly.   Here the intensity of labor
which enables Americans to underbid the English brings exhaustion to all concerned in it. In
this country workingmen are old at forty." (At
the meeting of the Federation of Labor I noticed the preponderance of young men.)   "It is
this all-possessing commercial spirit which has
put the claims of the Church to one side.
Against this the churches of the city are timid;
they have in them little brain or brawn, and no
grasp of the social life."   In his opinion, such an
environment had resulted in deadening the spirit
of self-sacrifice among ministers to such a degree that they scarcely knew what real self-
sacrifice was.   As the minister of a church in
the poor quarter he felt keenly his isolation, in
no respect more than in being regarded by some
as "an amiable lunatic" for choosing to remain with his church instead of accepting offers
from other churches of larger remuneration.
His comment was briefly: "As if the four Gospels didn't exist!"

This is the view of one man who has the
"psychological eye."   Another man, a gar-
ment-cutter and a member of a church — this

description would be almost adequate for identification — had practically the same view as
that of the minister I have just quoted. The
third man was a Roman Catholic priest, whose
eye I recognized as psychological as soon as
he turned it on me, and whose heart I knew to
be very human as soon as he had talked with
me five minutes. He frankly confessed to me
that he was " out of sympathy with the rich."
This from a man of commanding influence in
his Church. He gave me his explanation of
the failure of the Church to hold the workingman. He prefaced his remarks with a statement that even in Europe the poor are not to
be seen in the churches.

" The predominant vice of clergy, both Protestant and Roman Catholic, is ambition and
avarice. This shuts the poor out." Such was
the conclusion he had come to after years of
directing the Catholic missions to dependent
races in America. " State socialism is inevitable. What can the Church do to provide
for the people's material welfare ? Ever
since the Reformation the State has taken
over these former functions of the Church
— hospitals, schools, libraries, and the like.
When in need, the workingman used to

turn to the Church. Now he turns to the State. It's queer, very queer," he said, as he bade me good-by — and he spoke with feeling — " how little effect Christianity has upon us. The teachings of Christ, the Sermon on the Mount, the parables of Christ — we hear them, we preach them, but we don't practice them." And, with a Hibernian mixture of homely humor and serious and almost pathetic conviction, he added, " They are like water on a duck's back."

To pretend that these statements give a true impression of the general religious conditions of the city of Baltimore would be absurd. I hope I shall not be misunderstood in this respect. The churches in Baltimore are what may be called, in the ordinary understanding of the term, prosperous. One need only spend a Sunday there to be convinced that a great many people — perhaps an extraordinary proportion of them — attend the services of churches of all denominations. A large number of the churches of the city are doing great good in addition to the services of worship.[1] The old Church of St. Paul's Parish, antedating the founding of the

[1] A monograph on The Church and Popular Education was prepared by the late Professor Herbert B. Adams, of Johns Hopkins University, nearly one-half of which treats of the educational work of Baltimore churches.

city itself, has not only been a force in the city for generations, but still to-day, with narrowed boundaries and influence circumscribed by the rise of other churches, is doing an ever more widely varying work.   The charities of Balti-more, which owe their existence and maintenance to religious motives, are thoroughly well organ-ized; and, in spite of an unjustifiable criticism which I heard a workingman give upon them that they are chiefly for the exploitation of the sentimental rich, are wisely and humanly admin-istered.   But, to use the words of a member of St. Paul's Parish, an executive officer not only of the municipal but also of the national charity organization, "the relation between the work-ingman and the Church is not cordial; and it is the Church's fault."   That is equally true if in the word " Church " should be included all organized Christian bodies — even, I think I may say, the Salvation Army — and it is about equally true in all the larger cities of America, and in many of the smaller cities; less true in some, such as New Orleans, than in others, as, for example, St. Louis.

During my trip I met a number of ministers who had gained some reputation for success among workingmen.   In most cases I found the reputation resting on rather insecure foundation. As a rule, such success has been greatly magnified; or it has been temporary, originating in the excitement of some industrial agitation and ending with its subsidence; or else it has been a success, not with the great mass of self-respecting, progressive workingmen, but with the slum-dwellers.

Most Christian men, whether ministers or laymen, who have this matter at heart, feel, I think, dismayed at the condition. The fact that they are themselves so keenly aware of the chasm that separates the strong body of laboring men from the forces of organized Christianity makes them just as keenly sensitive to the callous and sometimes even complacent indifference concerning that chasm on the part of the membership of the churches. They recognize, too, that the labor organizations have preempted the ground which the churches otherwise might occupy; and even if the churches were eager to span that chasm, they do not know what diplomacy should be used for the purpose of getting a site on the other side for a pier for their bridge. The sincerely pious and churchly woman who devoutly kneels in her pew, serenely heedless of the fact that the stones of the church in which she worships, the wood on which she rests her head, the very prayer-book or hymnal she holds in her hand, were provided by men entirely untouched by the Church for which they had worked, is as near the solution of the problem as those men in whom serenity is impossible so long as the problem lasts.

Typical of those who know the problem, and are too disheartened or daunted to start solving it, was the Secretary of the Young Men's Christian Association at Richmond, Virginia. He was a native of Pennsylvania, and had been brought up in the labor districts of that State.

"Tackling the problem of 'working'" (he used the word in its religious sense) "among laboring men is very grave," was his opinion. "I've not done it, for I've not seen my way clear. It is very difficult to do anything with the laboring men except through their organizations. I am not sure that I want to identify myself with any labor organizations."

"The Christian Association recognizes that its religious work is to be done through the churches," I replied. "In regard to laboring men, might it not apply the same principles and work through labor unions?"

"That would be true," he said, "if it were

not for the fact that labor unions are often bitterly opposed to one another — as bitterly as
labor is opposed to capital — and I do not think
it is right for the Young Men's Christian Association to enter into these contentions."

" Are these contentions any bitterer than the
denominational fights which were even more
vehement when the Christian Association originated than now? And the Association has
never been involved in purely denominational
controversy."

"Perhaps not; but a great deal of tact and
care would be needed." And he left the
matter there, just about where everybody else
leaves it.

The Railroad Young Men's Christian Association is the only considerable organization
that I met with which is at all venturing to put
the religious life of workingmen into institutional form. Even when it is understood that
railroad men are an exceptional body of workingmen, separated in industrial organizations
and in class feeling almost as distinctly
from other workingmen as from capitalists,
still the success of the Railroad Young
Men's Christian Association certainly should
suggest to the Church at large some pos-

sible measures.   The Railroad Young Men's
Christian Association has shown itself to be
elastic in adapting itself to the peculiar conditions of a railroad man's life.   Instead of having
a theory and trying to make the men conform to it, it has studied the environment of the
men and conformed itself to that.   The train-
men must have one regular stopping-place besides their homes, at the other end of their route
or "run."   This fact has determined largely
the character of the Railroad Branch of the
Young Men's Christian Association.   To the
trainman it has aimed at being a second home.
To that end it has put foremost, or at least most
prominent, the comfort of its quarters; it has
provided smoking-rooms, for if it is to be his
second home it must be free from unnecessary
restrictions based on other people's notions of
what is expedient for him to do or not to do.
There he finds his time-tables; there he has a
bedroom; there he even receives his pay.   The
same liberal policy is adopted, I am told, in the
army and navy Associations.   As a result, the
members mentally associate the Christian spirit
with what in the minds of workingmen generally may be said to be their strongest ethical
motive — interest in the physical comfort and

welfare of the individual, the personal desire on the part of one man that another should be contented and happy. To the ordinary workingman "preaching the Gospel" at him conveys no impression of personal interest in him, on the contrary implies censure or at best condescension; but a comfortable substitute for a home away from home is to him evidence, certainly most convincing evidence, of an understanding of his point of view. It is putting the Gospel into his vernacular. At present "the whole state of Christ's Church" undoubtedly forbids the general adoption or adaptation of what is characteristic of the Railroad Young Men's Christian Association, but in some places it has been attempted with varying success.

In Mississippi I was waiting between trains at a station, when I noticed a dwelling-house designated by a sign as an Association of the Railroad Branch. I spent a few minutes in talking with the secretary and looking over the house. The office was in the smoking-room; the next room was a reading-room or parlor, in which the religious meetings were held; upstairs there were bath-rooms, and bedrooms very little but scrupulously clean. The town was a small one, too small to support more than one Association, and therefore this building answered for the use of the neighborhood as well as for the railroad. The secretary told me that the arrangement worked admirably, and that the freedom from restraint due to railroad influences seemed to give it a local advantage as well.

Of course the fact that the railroad corporations contribute to the financial maintenance of the railroad Associations gives occasion for prejudice against the Associations in the minds of the more bitter among the labor leaders; but this prejudice has not been effective enough to prevent an amazing growth. I imagine the men have much the same ideas about them as a man with whom I fell into conversation as I was going from Harrisburg to Reading, Pennsylvania. I found he was a watchman at a crossing; he had lost his legs in an accident, and was reduced by his disability to such simple work. His almost naïvely frank way of talking, and his calmly philosophic way of bearing the inevitable in his lot (he said, for instance, that at the time of his accident he never lost consciousness or worried in the least), gave to his opinions the more weight.

" The P. and R. didn't treat its men very

well till lately," he said in answer to a question of mine. "There were two or three accidents the past year or so. On that account all the old bosses were discharged, and now the bosses are all Young Men's Christian Association men and treat their men much better than the old bosses did. They all expect the men to do right. Yes, I'm an active member of the Young Men's Christian Association. I belong to the Hamburg Methodist Episcopal Church. Only two or three railroad men belong to that church. They say they are too restricted— can't go off from their homes and get drunk and have a good time. Drinking isn't the thing for a railroad man. Mr. Besler, superintendent of the road, is down on drinking. Some of the men like him and some don't. Then, you know, there are some men that want everything and aren't satisfied with that. The way I look at it, in the church everything is going to style. A poor man can't dress as well as a rich man, and his wife gets jealous because the other man's wife looks better than she does. Some men make fun of the churches and the Young Men's Christian Association, because you pay money in and don't draw any out for 'benefits.' "

"How would it be for the Young Men's Christian Association to have a benefit order ?"

"I don't know. It would be all right if they were all honest in the churches and the Young Men's Christian Association, but there are black sheeps in 'em all."

This frank-minded workingman, himself a member of a church and the Young Men's Christian Association, felt less distrust of a railroad corporation than of Christian institutions.

It is not my purpose to present theories concerning any phase of religion in America; but I cannot leave this subject of working people and the Church without setting down certain definite impressions made not merely by the experiences which are here recorded, but also by others for which I have not here the space. I wish I might give these other experiences in full; they would then be more convincing than they can be in the condensed form into which I am under the necessity of compressing them.

In the first place, the feeling of workingmen regarding not merely religion, but most specifically institutional Christianity, is not one of apathy. Apparent indifference must be accounted for otherwise than by attributing it to deep-seated apathy. Workingmen are indifferent to any presentation of the Gospel which is a theological statement, in either technical or popular terms, of a scheme by which a problematical soul may find entrance into a problematical heaven; they are equally indifferent to any presentation of practical religious conduct which amounts to the substitution of somebody else's conscience for their own. But they are not indifferent to religion itself, nor to the Church itself. A few questions, for instance, about religion, enough to suggest that somebody, supposedly identified with institutional Christianity, is interested in the religion of the workingman, were enough, I learned, to awaken the delegates of all the trades unions of a city to a quick and ingenuous response. The apathetic are not so easily aroused.

Then it may safely be said that the workingman is perfectly prepared to have religion deal directly and explicitly with the most perplexing and burdensome problems of his life. Throughout the course of my trip I was constantly meeting with this explanation of empty churches — that ministers deal too much with the "live issues" of daily life, which people want to forget, to have banished from their minds by the ministrations of the Church. The workingman will never go to church to forget his cares. He convinced me of that by telling me of his knowledge of other pleasanter and more effectual means. If he ever will go to church, it will be when the Church, through its ministers standing in the pulpits on Sundays, declares its acquaintance with his perplexities and its purpose not to gloze them and wheedle him into forgetting them, but to join with him in getting rid of their cause. The good news of a church set on ridding him of the evils he is suffering from would be a gospel he would be glad to hear preached.

Furthermore, at present a workingman is ill at ease in church; he feels there more than anywhere else the assertion of social distinctions. As he puts it, in the opera-house he can buy his right to a seat with money as good as anybody else's, or in a beer-garden he can buy as good drinks as anybody can for the sum he is willing to spend; but in a church — well, he is admitted on sufferance. And he feels these social distinctions quite as much in the missions as he does in the "fashionable churches" that support them. He would never support a Workingman's Theater; when he wants to see a play he is willing to go only to *the* theater. Just so he will be satisfied, not with a chapel, or even a " Workingman's Church," but only with The Church. To his thinking the Church Trust is an accomplished fact — well capitalized. This may be purely the figment of his imagination, but it is effectual in excluding him just the same. It is only reporting the substance of what has repeatedly been said to me to affirm that the only way in which this feeling of the workingman concerning the social aloofness of the Church can be removed is by the Church's forgetting its pride and proving itself by some positive action not guilty.

Moreover, this trait of social aloofness which the wage-earner attributes to the Church, so far as it exists — and it is not wholly a product of the imagination — is due less to ministers than to laymen. Clergymen are in general far more sensitive to the social and religious aspects of the labor problem, and are more in sympathy with the wage-earner, than are men and women whose views of the relation between employer and employed are likely to be distorted by self-interest. But ministers, convinced as they are of the purity of their own motives and those of the Church at large, seldom realize that promi-

nence in a church accorded to one or two
laymen of the smug and self-satisfied sort,
whose attitude to the laboring classes, so called,
is one of irritating patronage, is quite sufficient
to counteract all that the minister can say in
the pulpit, and all kindly fellow-feeling, little
appreciated because but little expressed, on the
part of the rest of the church.   It is prominence
rather than influence that makes the snobbish
well-to-do layman figure as the representative
of the Church in the mind of workingmen; just
as it is prominence rather than influence that
makes the irresponsible agitator figure as the
representative of workingmen in the mind of
many church people.

Still further: the ideas of the Church, and especially of ministers, which workingmen have,
have been formed from the reports of sermons
which appear in the newspapers.   Time and
again workingmen have said to me, "You don't
read in the papers of any ministers preaching
about this or that," or, "Such and such a view
is what the ministers teach, for I always read
the sermons in the Monday papers."

Here I may mention an illustration of the
erroneous impressions they are liable to receive
from this fact.   After my visit to the meeting

of the trades-union delegates, described in the foregoing chapter, a reporter interviewed me. The next day I bought a copy of his paper to see what he had said. There, in a conspicuous place, was a headline in heavy-face type, " No Religion," followed in smaller type by the words " Allowed to be Discussed at the Federation of Labor Meeting." From this entirely accurate statement of fact the conclusion was almost inevitable that the delegates showed antagonism to religion — a conclusion entirely at odds with the cordial interest they from first to last displayed. The one preacher in Baltimore who seemed to be universally popular among workingmen, I found by inquiry, had probably not a single workingman in his church. The most enthusiastic of his admirers with whom I talked had, I believe, never heard him preach. It was apparently only from the newspapers, in which his sermons often appeared, that the workingmen had any knowledge of him, and on his newspaper reputation his popularity among them almost wholly rested.

Without question, the standards which the workingman applies to institutional Christianity are largely materialistic. It does no good, however, to call his religion a Mud Philosophy and

dismiss it as such. Christianity is a seed; it
needs a soil. A cup of cold water is quite as
materialistic as anything the workingman
craves, and appears quite as unpromising in
spiritual results; but it sufficed as a test for
Christ to apply to his disciples. I was sorry to
find that the workingmen of Baltimore, like the
rest of mankind in general, were selfish in their
notions of religion. I found the question uppermost in their minds as they think of the Church
is the one more than once put to me, "What is
there in it for us?" I cannot see, however,
that that affords any reason for the Church to
turn away from them until they are of better
mind. If the Gospels are to be believed, this
same question was uppermost in the minds of
the twelve Apostles; but Christ accepted them
as material out of which to form his Church.

Of course, the question why the attitude of
the workingmen to the various forms of institutional Christianity should be so little one of
sympathy and so much one of alienation, not to
say hostility, is to a large degree a part of the
greater question why the Church and its allied
organizations find but little cordial response
from the masculine mind. The fact is well
known that among all classes of society women

form the majority of the constituents of the
Church. This condition is, moreover, by no
means distinctive of America. The congregations in the Roman Catholic churches of
Europe to all appearance show quite as small a
minority of male adherents as do the Protestant
churches of the United States. The fact, therefore, that men who are wage-earners in America
are not ordinarily found to be open allies of the
Church is only one aspect of a larger fact,
which, important though it is, I shall not discuss. It is an aspect, however, which has invited special attention, mainly because wage-
earners are organized as no other men are. It
is the organization of labor that has made the
relation between workingmen and the Church a
distinct phase of the religious life of America.

In Baltimore materialism is certainly in its
best estate — from its club dinners, which I
thankfully ate, to the financial health of its
charities. Surely material prosperity adorns
many virtues, such as hospitality (to this I
gratefully testify), and public spirit (witness
the city's many splendid monuments and beautiful streets), and piety (enriched with liturgy
and music); but also covers, in quite different
fashion from charity's way, a multitude of sins.

It was not mere chance that led me to find the problem of the separation between the Church and the workingman most representatively exhibited in the city of Baltimore. It is, therefore, to this aspect of religious life in Baltimore, rather than to other aspects more cheering and more typical of the city, that I have almost exclusively confined these two chapters.

The only apology I have to offer for devoting so large a proportion of this book to the relation between workingmen and the Church in Baltimore is that in my experiences the industrial problem impressed me as constituting a tremendous factor in the religious life of America in these days, and that in Baltimore I found conditions largely representative of conditions throughout the country. Further references to the subject in this book will be mainly incidental.

A VIRGINIA COUNTRY RECTOR

III

A VIRGINIA COUNTRY RECTOR

A LOCAL train running out from Richmond took me to Doswell. I knew it was only one chance in ten that I should be able to find the Episcopal minister I wanted to see. Certainly as I stood on the station platform and looked about on the wooded, level country, I could get but little encouragement. Off to the right about a quarter of a mile away were a few houses. Opposite the station was a store. The station agent, a young man, greeted me as if he were my host. Did he know Mr. Hepburn? He most cert'nly did know Rev. Hepburn; everybody did. Could he direct me to his house, and how could I go to it? Well, it was about five miles away along that road, and perhaps I could hire a horse at the store across the way. So across the way I went. Both horses

had gone to the mill.   Anywhere else to inquire?
No.   So I started afoot.   It was the latter part
of February.   The brown deadness of a Virginian winter intensified the effect of desolation
characteristic of a country suffering from ar-
rested development.   As I trudged along not
very cheerfully, I heard a shout behind me.   A
colored man was trying to attract my attention.
I waited while he walked leisurely up to where
I stood.   He offered to take me to Mr. Hepburn's.   I gladly made a bargain with him, and
off he started with some alacrity to get his
horse.   While he was gone I strolled over to
the neighboring house — or, more properly,
cabin.   From the small colored boy on the
porch I learned a little about the negro churches
in the neighborhood, but before I was well
under way my colored guide came driving
along at a furious pace.   Evidently he objected
to haste only when it involved exertion on his
own part.   As we drove away I talked with him
about the colored people.   From the information given by the driver and the boy I ascertained these facts: that there were two churches.
one Baptist, one Methodist; that almost all the
negroes were members of one or the other; that
there were no services except on Sunday; that

the minister of the Baptist church came up every Sunday from Richmond; that the minister was supported by what contributions he could get, not by any stipulated salary.

When we had gone a couple of miles, we saw a buggy coming toward us. It proved to contain Mr. Hepburn himself with his wife. I introduced myself. He had not received the letter of introduction which, I understood, was to have been sent him by one of his fellow-ministers. But he most cordially welcomed me and offered me, stranger as I was, the freedom of his house if I would drive on and wait for his return. I acquiesced in this hospitable proposal; but after he had gone I reversed my decision, as another plan occurred to me which might be more for his convenience as well as mine. This proved wise. I told my driver we would return to the station. Before we reached there we met Mr. Hepburn returning alone, his wife having taken the train to Richmond. The vacant seat beside him he offered to me, and I at once accepted it. Now he was free to make the pastoral calls he had planned, and I gained an hour more of his company.

The first impression he made on me was of strength, dignity, virility, and kindliness.

As he sat there erect with his blue military cape thrown over his shoulders yet not concealing the clerical coat-collar beneath, with the reins held taut in strong hands that seemed to respond with sympathetic control to every nervous movement of his high-strung horse, with his felt hat shading a pair of friendly eyes, his hair just tinged with gray, his chin strong and clean-shaven, his neck and face bronzed with exposure to the weather, he looked the very figure of what the minister of God in the Church militant should be.

For twenty years he had been traveling on this circuit in Virginia. Its boundaries had changed in the course of years. Now it covers a territory sixty miles long and eight miles wide, containing no villages whatever, only scattered houses. It is a region full of historic interest as the scene of the attack on Richmond. Within this parish he preaches regularly to six churches, in two of them every two weeks, in the others once a month. One of these churches is at Hanover Court-House, made famous by the Civil War.

In this circuit he had seen within twenty years a great social revolution. The character of the population has absolutely changed. He used to have for his congregation people of refinement. One in his congregation was a railroad manager, another was a judge of the Court of Appeals; there were lawyers and other men of high intelligence and education. Now this element of refinement is no longer dominant. He accounted for this change by referring to the introduction of electricity as the cause, which had so displaced the horse that the breeding of horses, which once was the source of wealth in the community, had ceased to be profitable. With the disappearance of wealth, leisure disappeared also: and with leisure went the opportunities for mental cultivation. Now the young people have to scramble for their living, and scrambling does not refine.

The first house we drove to in the course of the pastoral calls was a visible symbol of this vanished prosperity. Mr. Hepburn told me that it had been the mansion house of a Southern major and had been the scene of true old-time hospitality and gayety. Down below, where a level field lay brown and uncultivated, he pointed out to me the place where the training track had been. For all this I had to take his word. To my eye there was no sign of even a past greatness. My mind had formed an image of what a ruined Southern mansion and its place would look like, and, though the image was one of sadness, it was picturesque. On this February day there was nothing picturesque in the scene before me. It looked merely poor, unkempt, uninteresting. The present occupant of the house, an old, white-haired gentleman of no kin to the former owner, met us at the gate and bade us both welcome. Here he dwelt with his daughter. The wide, open hallway and the high-ceiled sitting-room were bare and scarcely furnished. There was no more sign of the past within than without. But the way in which the old, courtly gentleman and his gentle-voiced, fair-faced daughter entertained us, with the same courtesy and freedom from apology that they would have shown had their house been a palace, was a sign of the happier and easier past, the more pathetic because of the utter disappearance of all other signs. These people on whom the Episcopal minister made his pastoral call were Methodists.

From the old, time-disguised mansion we drove to a new and small house, where a son of the old major lives with his family. There he maintains the traditions of the family by

raising and training horses. The two negro
boys showed us with pride a few of the thor-
oughbreds. We then went to the house, where
the mistress graciously received us. Her two
young daughters were charming in their spontaneous welcome, not only to their old friend,
but also to me, a stranger. These parishioners
were "Campbellites," or, as they preferred to
be called, "Christians."

Leaving there, Mr. Hepburn turned his
horse's head toward home. Through the bare,
silent woods we drove, often over tree-stumps
left in the road itself. Sometimes Mr. Hepburn would wind his way among these stumps
as a skipper steers his vessel through a channel
full of reefs ; at other times he would "take"
a stump with a wheel as a boatman shoots a bit
of rapids; but always the masterful hands that
held the reins guided the horse with unerring
instinct. Once, as we went with a lurch into
what seemed to be a veritable morass, he turned
to me and said:

"You are not used, I reckon, to such a road
as this." It is impossible to reproduce his Virginian ways of speech that fell so pleasantly on
my Northern ears. "I should never get around
my parishes if I did not use such short cuts.

I've been driving over these roads for twenty years, and understand them by this time."

"Have you ever estimated the number of miles you have driven in the course of your duties?" I inquired.

"A lady once asked me that question, and I told her that I had driven around the world once and was well on my second journey. Ever since then each time she sees me she asks how far I've gone. The last time I told her that I was homeward bound near Wheeling on my third trip."

One would imagine that twenty years of such persistent labor among a people that had been declining all the time in wealth, leisure, and refinement might dismay and embitter him. Not so. On the contrary, his observation of conditions within the limits of his circuit had increased his hope and faith. True, with wealth had disappeared leisure; but in former days that leisure, he said, was used for the development not only of high and charming qualities in the Southern people, but also of moral weaknesses. It was, he said, the young man who had been brought up in idleness that, with his chivalry and courtesy, had also an uncontrolled passionate nature which found slavery providing objects for it, and had also the disinclination for useful work which results in shiftlessness and improvidence. Now with the new necessity for occupation there had come an improvement in character. In rural Virginia the mind of the young man of to-day is undoubtedly not so cultivated as the mind of the young man of twenty years ago, but his will is more efficient; he does not appreciate the amenities of life so well, but he values more highly its achievements. He has less suavity, more force.

As we turned into the highway and drove toward his home, Mr. Hepburn recounted an experience of his with a minister of the denomination popularly called " Campbellite." The man had come into this Virginia community from the West, and brought with him a breezy and aggressive spirit characteristic of his native place and his denomination. He began by a thoroughgoing effort to make proselytes. His field lay in one of Mr. Hepburn's parishes, and his influence was soon felt among some who were communicants in the Episcopal Church. His aim was to gather in a great number at a "baptism." The people of course attended his meetings in large numbers. Among those whom he had persuaded to be immersed were a number of young people whom Mr. Hepburn had baptized in infancy, some of whom indeed he, as a sort of practicing physician, had helped to usher into the world. This, Mr. Hepburn decided, should be stopped. So on one of his parochial, quasi-episcopal tours he called on this "Campbellite" minister to remonstrate with him for undermining the faith of these young people, however mistaken it might seem to him to be, and to give him fair warning that sturdy opposition would be made. Then Mr. Hepburn began a systematic visitation upon the families of all denominations. To those of his own Church he talked no more frankly than to the others. The Baptists he advised to consult with the Baptist minister; the Presbyterians to consult with the Presbyterian minister; and throughout he maintained his friendly relations toward the "Campbellites" themselves. The "Campbellite" minister endeavored to draw him into a public controversy, but in vain. When the "baptism" occurred at last, only six, instead of the twenty-eight advertised, were immersed, and these were gathered rightfully either from "Campbellite" families or from those outside of any church. So ended this unusual denominational fight for interdenom-

inational comity under the leadership of an
Episcopal minister!

"This is where I live," he said, as we turned
in at a gate. The road led to a large, old-
fashioned house. On either side it was flanked
with a row of little one-story cottages. It seemed
as if the old house were reaching out its arms
with hospitable welcome as we drove up under
the trees to the high, wide porch. The place
once was Hanover Academy. The old house
was the home of the head master. The little
cottages, containing a couple of rooms apiece,
were the dormitories for the boys. In the back-
ground, standing in the middle of a plowed
field, I caught a glimpse of the school-house,
now fast falling into decay. Once upon a time
Thackeray was a guest here.

While we waited for luncheon to be prepared
we chatted together before the open fire in the
library. Library I call it, but it contained only
one small book-case filled with rather old-
fashioned books. Mr. Hepburn studies mainly
in the open air; most of his books are living
people, and much of what he reads is, after
these twenty years, what he himself has written
in their lives.

After a luncheon of fine Virginia ham and

rice, he took me out to show me his farm, for he raises a large part of what he needs in his own household.   He has a few negro servants. In one of the outbuildings was his workshop, with carpenter's bench and blacksmith's forge. There he showed me a sort of derrick he had made with his own hands for lifting invalids from their beds.   It was now, as he remarked, itself invalidated by the introduction of trained nurses.   All his life he had done a great deal of manual labor.   He used, for instance, to cobble the shoes for his family.

The colored stable-boy brought to the door a beautiful thoroughbred mare, the gift of a friend of Mr. Hepburn's, harnessed to the light buggy in which he made his pastoral tours. We started off to drive over a part of his circuit.   Our talk drifted to the negroes who lived in the region.

" They won't let me do any religious work among them," he told me, " not even preach for them.   But they often call upon me to cure their sick and even to pull teeth for them."

" Have you studied medicine? " I inquired.

" You see, there is no professional physician in a region like this," and he swept with his hand an arc of the horizon.   We were several miles from the railroad station. "So," he continued, "for the sake of my own family, I had to acquaint myself with the use of medicine. Then the families in my parishes would call me in in cases of emergency. So I've come to be a sort of physician as well as a minister. I have even had to do surgical work. I don't know how many children and young people there are in my parishes at whose birth I have attended.

"See how free that mare is! She will go like that all day — and day after day. She will take me forty or fifty miles and she will keep her gait to the last mile. To the end it will be all I can do to hold her. It is endurance that shows a thoroughbred. Do you notice that one of her hips is higher than the other? That is how she happens to belong to me. But it makes no difference for my purposes. We Virginians admire anything that is thoroughbred."

This explicit expression of his joy in the genuine was implicit in all that he said. Admiration for whatever is sterling was a part of his religion.

He told me a story which showed that his knowledge of horses had still another bearing upon his work as a minister. He was once asked to participate in the dedication of a monu-

ment in Richmond. On the morning of the day
set for the dedication he was to perform a mar-
riage ceremony a number of miles from the city,
where he could make no connections by train.
He calculated his chances of reaching the city
on time and accepted the invitation. He explained to the committee of arrangements that
he could not be present to join the procession at
its formation, but he could meet the procession
at a certain point and go from there to the
monument. On the committee was a judge who
was known to be irreligious, and rather scornful
of ministers; he laughed at the notion that any
minister should be man of affairs enough to
keep an appointment under such circumstances.
When the day came, Mr. Hepburn went to the
wedding, performed the ceremony, and then, by
using a relay of horses, rode to the place of
appointment, reaching it punctually, joined the
procession, and made the prayer of dedication.
The judge was so impressed with this demonstration of the truth that a Christian minister
could be a man that, for the first time in his
life, he gave serious thought to religion, and before he died became a declared Christian.
"All because," Mr. Hepburn explained, "I
knew the capabilities of a horse."

So scattered is the population that religious life lacks almost every social element, even the most common, except, of course, the gathering of congregations for worship on Sunday. No "church sociables" are held; and no clubs aside from one or two missionary societies exist in connection with any of his churches.

His circuit includes two large parishes, St. Martin's and St. Paul's. Within these two parishes are six churches, four in one parish, two in another. In two of these six churches, as I have said, he preaches once in two weeks, in the others once a month. The churches of other denominations within the limits of these parishes are also on circuits, and conflict of services is regularly avoided; so that on the Sunday he preaches in any church he has a congregation made up practically of the whole neighborhood. Consequently he preaches regularly to people of other denominations. In one church he has fifty Episcopal communicants out of a total of eighty people; in another fifty out of a total of one hundred; in another fifteen out of a total of seventy-five. In the latter church, for instance, he has not a single male communicant; but people of all the denominations participate in the church service. The organist is a Bap-

tist, the choir leader and Sunday-school superintendent a Presbyterian. The offering is received by a Methodist and a Baptist. But of
all his churches that is the one which has the
most churchly service, and that is where the
responses are clearest and most enthusiastic.
He feels that there more than anywhere else he
is expected to conduct the service with dignity
and scrupulous adherence to the Prayer-Book.
The men who bring forward the offering perform their duty with the utmost care. All work
in perfect accord. Even in the Mite Society,
whose funds are of course turned into Episcopal
channels, only two of the members are Episcopalians.

Mr. Hepburn made it apparent that he had
very clear conceptions of the duty of the Episcopal Church in such a community. In certain
respects, he was free to confess, the Methodists
and Baptists might reach more people by means
of the emotional elements in their religion; but
it seemed to him that those very emotional elements resulted in religious instability. He con-
ceived that it was his distinctive duty to stand
for orderliness and dignity in religion, for its
permanency, its higher ideals, and its vital
obligations.

As the church just described illustrates the friendliness that existed between the Episcopalians and the other denominations, so another church of which he spoke illustrates the distinctive function of the Episcopalians in this country region. This church is in a neighborhood where the other denominations have had constant trouble with the hoodlum element; but in his church, Mr. Hepburn told me, he has had no trouble whatever. He ascribed this to the simple dignity of the service. The boys that sit around the stove quietly disperse as soon as he appears with his surplice in the chancel. Once he invited the clerical club of his part of the State to meet at that very church. He knew that this would bring a great crowd of the country people there, and for once he anticipated some trouble. The church was packed, and he saw that some of these boys were restless. He thereupon selected a few of the more troublesome and made them monitors. There was absolutely good order. I gathered not only from this fact, but also from some stories that were told me about his experiences with such congregations, that his own personal dignity and tact, as well as the liturgy of his Church, were effectual for good order.

In one of his congregations Mr. Thomas Nelson Page, who, it is hardly necessary to say, represents not only literary but aristocratic distinction in Virginia, is a regular attendant. On Sundays, therefore, especially in summer, Mr. Hepburn faces a congregation of which the front row consists of such members of the "F. F. V.s," and immediately behind them people who can neither read nor write.

"How do you preach to a congregation of that sort?" I inquired.

"Well," he replied, with a laugh, "I preach at the second row."

We came to a turn in the road, and there under the trees stood a little old brick church. Quaint, square, bulging brick pillars supported the little porches, one in front and one at the side. An old brick wall with rounded top inclosed the churchyard.

"It is the Old Fork Church," he said.

He tied his horse to a tree, went to the side porch, leaned down, and took a big brass key from under the step.

"Everybody knows it is kept here," he remarked.

The church was built about 1735, and has been in constant use ever since. It still stands

the venerated sacred place of the vicinity, full
of historic associations, not only religious, but
civil and military. During both the Revolutionary and Civil Wars it was occupied by the
soldiers. It has seen one sect after another
rise and spread throughout the region, and yet
remains the sanctuary for people of all creeds
and of no creed at all. The interior was
strangely unlike an Episcopal church. In the
middle of the front wall rose stiffly an old-
fashioned wine-glass pulpit. In front of the
pulpit stairs on one side was the reading-desk
(it could hardly well be called a lectern); in
front of the stairs on the other side stood the
prayer-desk. Between these two, and directly
in front of the pulpit, stood what Mr. Hepburn
said "no one would call an altar, I reckon —
it is a sure-enough table according to the Ru-
brics." Before the communion-rail, which was
such as one might see in any country Methodist
church, stood on a standard a simple marble
font. How old this font is is not exactly known,
but it antedates the Baptist uprising in Virginia.
Even at that troublous time the church itself
was unharmed; but this font with its standard
was carried away by the Baptists in protest
against what they thought a false and perni-

cious doctrine. For years it was lost, but at last it was discovered in a cellar, being used as a receptacle for meat. The standard has apparently irretrievably disappeared; so now the font rests on a wooden standard painted in imitation of marble — the only suspicion of pretense I noticed during my whole day's experience. The wooden pews, the warped old communiontable, even the little wooden foot-stools, are the very ones originally placed in the church, and they remained without paint or varnish until the first year of the twentieth century, when the ladies of the church painted the interior with their own hands.

It was with reluctance that I left this little old church. As I got my last glimpse of it at a turn of the road it seemed to be an interpreter of Virginian rural life. In the midst of this country region, apparently so undeveloped as to seem to be new and unsettled, this church stood as a monument to a noble past, a repository of its best traditions, and a symbol of the reverence and hope of the present.

Before Mr. Hepburn left me at the station he took me to one other of his churches. It was a simple, unpretentious wooden structure, apparently containing nothing noteworthy. Mr.

Hepburn, however, called my attention to a memorial tablet. The man to whose memory it was erected had regularly visited and addressed the Sunday-school for a long term of years, although he was a Baptist; and so it happens that this memorial to a Baptist stands in an Episcopal church.

If in the course of my trip my observations had led me to fancy that institutional Christianity was only another phase of human selfishness and display, and that religion itself was but a part of sociology, this one day's experience would have been enough to convict me of folly. The Episcopal Church is known to stand among Protestant bodies distinctively for the claims of institutional religion, and is sometimes charged with selfishness, more often with display. That these qualities are not integral parts of institutional religion even in its most pronounced form, the life of this Virginian rector is abundant proof. Where reverence needed to be quickened he has brought the dignity of public worship; where consciences needed to be touched he has brought the prod of plain speech; where he has been able neither to preach nor to lead in worship, he has been ready to serve in the guise of a physician; he has been

ready to take any path to the human heart,
though it were the heart of a self-ostracized
negro, and the path led by the devious way of
pulling teeth! So much for selfishness and display. And as to sociology, it would be pretty
hard to find it in the religious work of a minister whose people are thinly scattered over a
territory of four hundred and eighty square
miles.

In the last analysis, every successful religious
work that I have seen can be attributed to the
same causes that have made Mr. Hepburn's
work in a high degree successful — the impact
of a dominant personality. Doctrines, organizations, methods, have been the creatures, not
the creators, of any religious life I have had
the chance to observe. The creator has always
been a person. In this case the personality of
Mr. Hepburn, though comparatively unaided,
was also comparatively untrammeled.

Such a life as Mr. Hepburn's is not unique
in Virginia. In fact, with change of personality and location, it is duplicated all through the
South. One rector in the city of Richmond
told me that early in his ministry he had a
similar rural parish. His church was in the
center of population, and there were preaching

places eight, ten, thirteen miles away in different directions. Most of his time, he told me, he spent on horseback. And this was his testimony as to the hopefulness of Southern rural life: " There is in the main no sign of moral or religious degeneracy. Nine-tenths of the theological students come from rural parishes. In the parish I had, six men out of fifty communicants have gone into the ministry since I left, eighteen years ago — and it was not a remarkable parish either.

Another rector in Richmond told me that his first experience in the pastorate was in circuit-riding, all in connection with negroes; and that it involved all sorts of work — going into their cabins, giving them orders on stores, providing them with medicines, and praying with them.

I have mentioned these Episcopal ministers because I think it is generally believed that circuit-riding is peculiar to the Methodists. As a matter of fact, I found it common in all the denominations in the South. This fact was impressed upon me in conversations it was my privilege to have with several students at Richmond College, one of whom was a minister's son from Georgia, another from Florida, another a resident, I believe, of one of the Carolinas. They all told me the same story of circuit-riding. In the course of one of these conversations I heard of one village of five hundred inhabitants — and this goes to show that circuit preaching is not confined to the sparsely settled country regions — which had five churches of different denominations, each with a preacher of its own. Not one of these preachers lived in the village. One had his home in the country about ten miles away, the others all had their residence in the city of Richmond. This village was simply a part of their circuits. And yet some Sundays every church was closed. There at least there seemed to be lacking the saving power of the right personality.

The student from Florida was the son of a Baptist minister, in whose circuit was the Baptist church of Tallahassee, the capital of the State. At first he lived outside of Tallahassee and came periodically to preach in the city. Gradually the church grew, until, now that it had a membership of seventy-five, he had moved to Tallahassee, but had retained charge over a church in another place. He was still a circuit preacher, with his headquarters in the capital of the State.

Nothing could better illustrate the fact that in the South rural conditions largely preponderate. And if the country rector of whose life I had a glimpse is typical of rural ministry in the South, as I have good reason to believe, there is justification for the hopefulness which I found to be a Southern characteristic.

RELIGIOUS TENDENCIES OF
THE NEGRO

IV

RELIGIOUS TENDENCIES OF
THE NEGRO

IT is not my purpose either to add to the already numerous descriptions of the picturesque in the religious life of the negroes in the South, or to attempt any final answer to questions concerning the nature of their religion, but simply to relate some of the experiences that came to me as the result of two queries: First, In what direction and to what point has the best in the negroes' religious life been developing? Second, What do the Southern white people think, not only of the negroes' religion, but also of the relation between their own religion and the race problem?[1]

[1] With regard to the latter question I wish to call attention to "Race Problems of the South : Report of the Proceedings of the First Annual Conference held under the auspices of the Southern Society for the Promotion of the Study of Race Conditions and Problems in the South " (B. F. Johnson Pub. Co., Richmond, Va., 1900). Of these addresses, given from widely various points of view, several present the religious aspects of the race problem. The more hopeful and courageous of these addresses are more representative of the opinions of the people of the South I talked with than the two or three that are pessimistic and fearful.

Naturally, in looking for signs of progress I gave my attention chiefly to the negro churches of the cities. If, like the casual traveler, I had gone only to the churches where both in numbers and in "character" the congregations would seem to be most typical of the colored people, I should have found little evidence of progress. In the cities of the South the great mass of negroes flock together in huge churches which often number two or three thousand members each. The chief service on Sunday is held in the evening, when the colored people are free from their work, which is largely menial. One Sunday evening in Charleston, South Carolina, I attended service at one of these churches. The church was Methodist. The building was crowded. The congregation was singing a hymn as I entered. Beneath the quavering appoggiaturas that rose and fell at the pleasure of individuals in all parts of the congregation like the spray from waves dashing over shoals, I recognized with difficulty an old familiar psalm tune. An aged "mammy" in a pew ahead of me was swaying back and forth, with her eyes half closed. Here and there throughout the congregation others were swaying in the same rhythmic fashion. The hymn was ended; the excitement was only begun. On the platform were half a dozen negro ministers. One came forward and offered prayer. More and more fervent he became; more and more he pounded the pulpit. Inarticulate cries and shrieks rose from the pews. The prayer ended, then came the first of the collections; there were three before the end of the service. Another minister preached the sermon. He began colloquially, referring a great deal to himself. Then he urged certain moral precepts. Before long he was as wrought up as his audience; and finally, with hoarse and screaming voice, he described in imagination his progress across Jordan, up the golden streets, straight to where in the center on one throne sat the Father, to his right on another sat the Son, and to the left on still another sat the Holy Ghost, whereupon, with a shout, " I'm here at last! " he cast himself upon the very throne itself — not merely in imagination, for, amid the frenzy of the audience, he flung himself into one of the pulpit chairs with his legs crossed wildly in the air.

I had an experience almost paralleling this when I went to a negro prayer-meeting in the heart of the city of Atlanta, Georgia. There, after the minister had finished his shouting and

gesticulating, the assembled negroes fell upon
their knees, and then one of the number, a burly
negro with a brutal face, chanted or rather intoned on two high notes a sort of barbarian lit-
any, accompanying himself by rhythmically
clapping his hands and pounding the bench in
front of him. His words were hardly distin-
guishable for the moaning of those all about me,
which resembled nothing so much as the lowing
of a great herd of cattle.

It is such exhibitions of uncontrolled and arti-
ficially aroused emotion that are referred to in
most generalizations about negro religion. But
it is to be remembered that even in these pronounced cases there was evidence of a strong
tendency away from mere emotionalism. The
preacher in Charleston felt it necessary to spend
a good part of his sermon in very plain speaking concerning moral conduct; and the matter
of the address made by the Atlanta preacher at
the prayer-meeting, however violent his manner,
had direct bearing on the lives of his people.
And Dr. Du Bois, of Atlanta University, whose
published studies of the conditions of his race
have entitled his testimony to great weight, told
me that all such churches give similar evidence
of two factors: one, the old-style darky whose

religion is of the hallelujah order; the other, the younger generation who are ashamed of these emotional outbreaks. The younger element is, of course, finally going to control. And one especially hopeful fact is to be noted: partly because the church is for the negroes their one racial rallying place, partly because the negroes have been born and bred in a community where among the whites church-going is the rule, not the exception, the great mass of negro working people go to church. I found it generally safe to assume that the colored porter or waiter or driver whom I happened to speak to was an attendant, almost always a member, of a church. Whatever advance, therefore, is to be seen in the colored churches is indicative of an advance made by at least the respectable part of the race abreast.

At Tougaloo, Mississippi, where there is a "university" for negroes, the influence of wise religious education was very perceptible. In that country community, where still negroes ask of their Northern teachers assurance that the earth is not round in order to keep their faith in the Bible that speaks of the "corners of the earth," where still many negroes, young and old, are strongly confirmed in their belief that before "getting religion" a person must feel the devil depart from some one or other definite part of his anatomy, where still a young negro man recently did not know it was wrong for his pastor to have two wives, I attended services in two colored churches, both Baptist. In each the service was perfectly orderly and devout. The preacher in one church, with rich negro dialect, made a very thoughtful and appealing address. The course of his thought was something like this: God is love. If you are a Christian and have religion, you have God in your heart; therefore you have love in your heart. But if you loved one another you would not be dishonest; we could trust you with our daughters and our wives. The colored people especially need to love one another, because they have no leaders. In the other church the sermon, evidently on Job, was drawing to a close. The " elder " was indicating from the experience of the man of Uz that Christians are not free from the attacks of Satan.

After the service I talked with a colored farmer-preacher, with the " elder " and others, one after another. They were unanimous in saying that the colored people of the neighborhood had improved morally and materially. They gave much credit to the university. One of them, a former gambler, told how the gambling and the demoralizing horse-racing had been done away with, not by violent reform, but by the change of the character of the colored people themselves. As the "elder" said, "We is progressing very fast." My driver, a young colored man of twenty-two who modestly expressed his ambition to be a minister, said that even in his short experience he had noted an improvement toward quietness and good order.

A type of negro church much higher than the Charleston church I have described was one in Baltimore in which I attended a preaching service. The Christian Endeavor meeting which preceded the preaching service showed no trace whatever of emotionalism; indeed, except in one or two particulars, its success in imitating the most perfunctorily respectable meeting of white "Endeavorers" was almost perfect. The service in the church, on the other hand, was decidedly ejaculatory; although the use of the decalogue, partly intoned in a crude way, with "gospel hymns" intercalated among the responses, indicated an effort to give dignity to the service. The sermon, which began as a sketch of the history of the denomination, ended with a series of loosely joined but fervently expressed appeals to race pride, and very candid and explicit exhortations to moral rectitude on the part of the young people. When, after the service, I spoke to the minister, his race-consciousness changed pitifully from the self-assertive form to the apologetic; and when two days later I called on him in his home, where tokens of his race-consciousness in the form of portraits of colored church dignitaries hung on the walls to the exclusion of all other pictures, my interview was very unsatisfactory; the frankness of his public speech was gone; because I was a white man I did not have his confidence. The ethical questions he had raised in his sermon he dismissed by saying that the cure for all evils among whites as well as blacks was to "preach Christ and practice what you preach." Like many another man face to face with a big problem, he was willing to accentuate its difficulties in justifying himself and others in the same condition, but when it came to analyzing the problem and discussing methods of solution he was content with a generalization.

In the movement away from an emotional religion unrelated to conduct, the churches I

have mentioned were evidently not leaders but
followers. They therefore represent a much
larger number of the colored people than the
churches I shall describe in the rest of this
chapter. These, I think, may roughly be
divided into two classes: those which believe
that the emotional character of the negro ought
not to be suppressed, but educated and guided;
and those which believe that that emotional
character should be minimized by the magnifying of the intellectual and ethical.

To the former avowedly belongs the very
ritualistic Episcopal mission church for negroes
in Baltimore called St. Mary's. It is in the
negro quarter, near Mount Calvary Church,
which sustains it. I found my way into the
church one afternoon. The interior was rather
dingy. The altar with its candles was elabo-
rate. Around the walls were the pictures of
the Stations of the Cross, such as hang on the
walls of Roman Catholic churches. On one of
the benches lay a ragged negro boy asleep. As
I went to the place where an image of the
Virgin stood, he roused, and, in answer to my
inquiry, told me where I might obtain information regarding the mission. At the clergy-
house, to which he directed me, the chief im-

pression I received from the white ministers in
charge was of their recognition of the moral
significance of their work.   In place of the un-
restrained appeal to the emotions which the
Baptists and Methodists made by revivals, they
hoped to substitute a regulated appeal by means
of the liturgy of the High Church service, with
its incense, its lights, its music directed to
moral ends.   And in the confessional, they
were convinced, they had a means by which the
religion of the individual negro could be connected in a very personal and direct way with
repentance from sin and instruction in righteousness.   Both from my observation and
from the testimony of High Church Episcopalians and Roman Catholics I am persuaded that
this appeal has had but little effect; and whatever success it has had is confined almost exclusively to the more ignorant negroes, who
are most unlikely to lead in the development of
the race.

As a rule, the Episcopalians of the South do
not favor the ordination of colored men to the
priesthood, though there is a strong minority
that desires it.   In the course of my trip I personally met two colored rectors.   One, the rector of a small ritualistic church in Charleston,

I found getting ready for a rehearsal; he teaches his choir the Gregorian music by ear. The other I met in Baltimore, where he is rector of a church neither high nor ritualistic.

While searching for the colored rector in Baltimore, I called on a barber who was a member of his church — St. James's. I found him in his shop. His appearance, bearing, and manner had all the pronounced characteristics of a gentleman of the old school. He was full of enthusiasm for his church, proud of the fact that St. James's was the oldest colored vestry and the only independent colored vestry in Maryland, proud of the pamphlets and reports that it had published, proud of its rector, proud of the orphanage it was maintaining. I inquired whether the churches were merely standing for emotional religion, or helping to create character. His reply had at least the merit of discrimination:

" That involves," he said, " a mental separation of those who are native from the inroads of Virginia negroes. On the whole there is improvement. What is more, there is increasing confidence among the white people in the colored race. For instance, the trustees of the St. James orphanage, called the Maryland

Home, all colored men, had no experience, but every one of them was a business man — yes, I am one of the trustees. They appealed to the charitable public and were supported from the beginning. There is increasing confidence, too, among the colored people in the educated men of their own race. They are readier now than formerly to go, for instance, to colored physicians. As a matter of fact, it all lies within the individual; he has power to create confidence."

In further search for the colored rector of St. James's, I called first at the rectory, which bore no such obtrusively assertive marks of race-consciousness that I had noted in the house of the colored Methodist minister; then at the printing-office where this rector prints with his own hands what is a combined parish paper and church calendar, and also the circulars and a weekly paper for his church orphanage; then at St. James's Church, a small church, smudgy within and without, on a sunless side street; finally at the orphanage, where I found him. He was small, clean-shaven; his face was full of sparkle and animation; his mind was overflowing with ideals and schemes. In this home for friendless colored children was

tangible evidence that his energy was efficient.
He showed me over the building — an ordinary
city house adapted for its present use, scrupulously clean. The children, some of them
picked up from ash-heaps and gutters, were in
charge of a colored kindergartner; they showed
clearly the fruits of discipline and good care.
In the meanwhile he talked with great animation, not only about his own work, but as well
about the practical problems of the race. The
fact that the Episcopal Church among the colored people was composed of the better-paid
and better-educated class made it difficult, he
said, to reach the "masses"; for the negroes
have very well-defined class distinctions among
themselves. At the same time this fact does
not bring specially vigorous financial support
to the Church. He illustrated it thus: Eliza
gets twelve dollars a month, and gives one
dollar to the Church. She jumps into a position yielding fifty dollars. At once she finds
herself in a new circle of life; she knows more
about balls and parties, more of the require-
ments of dress, of reading, of a multitude of
things she never had before. So she still pays
one dollar to the Church. Her rise seems to be
away from her religion; it seems so because

her life now radiates in so many more directions. In this way the material progress of the race, he explained, does not bring proportionate prosperity to the Church; and so far from deploring it, he seemed to take joy in the financial burdens he had to bear, so long as they were brought upon him by an increasingly radiating life for his people. He believed thoroughly in colored ministers for colored churches; colored teachers for colored pupils; colored leaders for colored people. The existence of white ministers over colored congregations encourages the already too great characteristic of dependence in the negro race, he maintained, and it should be recognized by Northerners who are doing religious and charitable work among the negroes. As he put it, "We want their advice, not because it is white, but because it is right." He was frank enough to say, in giving a further reason for this, that colored people under white supervision feel irresponsible, and often prefer white supervision in order to be relieved of responsibility, for "no colored man finds it possible to speak with the unreserved friendliness to a white man that he would use in speaking to one of his own race."

In this he was strangely confirmed by what

the priest who is the head of the Catholic Missions to Negroes and Indians remarked to me. Although an Irishman, he was the most vigorous partisan of the negro I met in the course of my trip. "It is significant," he said, "that everything that has been done against the negro has turned out to his advantage: the Missouri Compromise, the Ku Klux Klan, the War against the Union, and now negro disenfranchisement. It is not surprising that no white man has the confidence of the negro. Why, I have worked among them for years, and yet a young negro who comes fresh into this seminary will know more in a day about the colored people whom I come in contact with than I am able to find out in a lifetime. It is hard to persuade the Catholic Church to ordain negroes to the priesthood; but we must have them. That we have not is due to race prejudice; but to show how unreasonable and inconsistent that prejudice is, these same people that object to negro priests took up a little while ago the fad of going to confession in Washington to a regular corn-field nigger priest."

In reply to my inquiry whether colored choirs could be trained to sing the Gregorian music, he replied:

"Colored churches don't need choirs. You know the proverb we have, God Almighty at one end of the church and the devil at the other. Well, it doesn't apply to them. The negro has his own music, and it's an ornament to his character."

In Washington I called on Dr. J. L. M. Curry, Agent of the Peabody and Slater Funds. I found him immersed in a mass of correspondence, and very busy. When I stated to him that my errand was to look into the religious conditions of the South, he interjected between directions to his private secretary, "Well, young man, if you are going South to study the nigger question, you might just as well start for the moon." Nothing could better illustrate the fact that every problem in the South seems to the Southerner to be the race problem; and incidentally that the Southern people, even the most patient and catholic, have become wearied of the long years in which they have borne the inroads of self-complacent Northerners with theories about the negro. On the other hand, when I stated more fully my purpose and presented letters of introduction from The Outlook, Dr. Curry's cordiality was unbounded; he left his pressing work to give me such invaluable information and assistance as only his wide experience and liberal mind could give. This was typical of my experience in the South. One young Southerner left his office and spent hours with me, urging with hot, impetuous language the immediate necessity for the education of the negroes. His nervous energy seemed to justify his optimism, too. Through him I got a glimpse of that not inconsiderable number of young Southern men who are putting their minds and their strength into the solution of the race problem, not with academic theories, but with practical determination and with joy in the conflict that would gladden the heart of a Roosevelt or a Riis. He spoke highly, by the way, of the work that the Presbyterian Church is doing to give the negroes religious training out of their usual emotionalism.

The lowly, compassionate Jesus, who ate with publicans and sinners and did not hesitate to talk with a Samaritan woman, has no sincerer and more truly democratic followers than the Christian people of the South. No inquiry into religious conditions of America could easily omit the query, What do these Southern Christians say to the social ostracism of the black race? That was a question I found it difficult, as a Northerner, to propound without a tone of seeming self-righteousness. Ask it I did, however, with as much candor and tact as I could. Two answers I think it worth while to report. One was from a Methodist minister of Virginia. At first he was rather reticent, but volunteered to say, "What phase are you seeking for?" and then added, "We give contributions for the support of colored churches, and have a kindly feeling for the race. The South understands the negro better than the North, and treats him better," and so forth in the usual strain.

"But how about the practical side of their life? Clerkships, for instance?"

"Why, they can have them in their own stores," he replied magnanimously, "but not in white stores. The thinking portions of the race do not want such positions and would be uncomfortable in them. So with social position," and he cited Booker Washington, with strong praise.

"But," I persisted, "if a man should attempt personally to practice Christ's precepts by mingling with the colored people?"

"He would be cured in a week, not only by ostracism, but by flooding himself with a lot of negroes physically, socially, and morally offensive."

That the sacrifices thus involved might be a part of the discipleship of Christ did not seem to be worth considering by this minister. He later gave a more plausible reason when he likened social equality for the negro to a razor in the hands of a child.

The other answer was given by a lady of great personal charm, of profoundly democratic convictions and sympathies, who belonged by right of inheritance and of personal experience more to the South as a whole than to any one State:

" The attitude of the Southern people toward the negro would be defended by the Southern Christian on the ground that it was for the best good of the negro. To recognize socially a cultivated negro and his wife would work an injury to the colored race by creating false expectations on the part of the unfit. Moral brotherhood is recognized, but not equality; the relation of helper to helped, but not the relation of reciprocity."

Except in the Roman Catholic churches of the South, it is very rarely that negroes worship in the same churches with the whites. This was not the case before the war, I was told, in many parts of the South. A Baptist church of Charleston still reserves, according to its ante-bellum custom, one gallery for colored people. It is usually well occupied, and their rights are scrupulously maintained by the church, even when the seating capacity is taxed to its utmost. Most of the colored people who attend are members of colored churches, but they come to the service in this white church because they feel that they are getting from the preaching there something which they could not get from their own ministers.

With one of the colored Baptist ministers of the city I had an interview. His chief concern about his people was for their education. As he said, "It is hard to make good Christians of them when they are ignorant." He was there-fore maintaining a school for negroes, modeled in a humble way after Tuskegee. He spoke with dignified intensity of the low moral condi-tion of the negroes in Charleston. "Every time I get a chance I talk about it, though the colored people don't like to hear about it. Yes, licentiousness too." When I saw him he had just had a revival in his church, and he was giving his attention to the young converts by

14896

trying to give them something to do. He complained, however, that there was no way of setting them to work because they were ignorant. He thus reverted to the supreme need of education.

One gentleman with whom I talked had the distinction of being at the same time a Southerner through and through, the son of a slave-owner, and the head of an institute maintained by the Methodist Church South for the higher education of negroes. As a young man, I was told by one who knew him well, he felt the burden of the ignorance of the newly freed slaves, and, sacrificing the life of refinement for which he had pronounced taste, and facing probable ostracism, he took up the burden. As a matter of fact he has not been ostracized, though necessarily isolated. After years of experience it was his deliberate opinion, expressed in his conversation with me, that although most of the Southern white people know the traits and general character of the mass of the colored people better than the people of the North could possibly know them, they were utterly unacquainted with the growing class of educated negroes, knew nothing of their manner of life, their attainments, their

ambitions, their religion. Whatever intimacy
there has been in the past between the races
has been that growing out of the relation of
servant to master. Wherever that relation has
ceased the intimacy has disappeared. As a
consequence the significant improvement in the
religious life of the negroes is coming, like
the rest of the kingdom of heaven, not with
observation.

The church which, better than any other I
happened upon, represents those leaders of the
negroes who are guiding the race away from a
merely emotional religion, was a colored Congregational church of Atlanta. Without exception, white or black, it was apparently the
most progressive and best organized church I
saw in the South. The minister is a graduate
of Fisk University and Yale Divinity School.
Connected with the church is a Men's League,
resembling somewhat a "lodge" without se-
crecy or insurance, a Literary Society, which,
as I happened casually to see it at one of its
meetings, resembled such a literary society as
might be found in a New England town, and a
Young People's Society. But the distinguishing characteristic of the church is the fact that
the whole church itself is organized into what

are called Circles of Help.   Each circle consists
normally of ten members, every one of whom
has a distinctive duty.   Number one in each
circle is chairman, through whom the circle receives the pastor's directions; number two is
assistant chairman; number three keeps the
records and corresponds with absent members
of the circle; number four, the treasurer, is responsible for raising church funds within his
circle; number five promotes the devotional
life; number six promotes social life, and especially drives off the demon of sanctimony;
number seven sees that attention is given to
the sick; number eight sees that members visit
one another; number nine sees to the relief of
poverty; number ten is general promoter of
new methods.   The minister receives monthly
reports from the circles, and when I talked
with him was planning to have an occasional
meeting of the same "numbers," all the
"sevens," for instance, for the consideration
of their special work.   Although the church
has barely four hundred members, it is far
more influential than some of the negro churches
with a membership of two or three thousand.

During my visit at Atlanta I had occasion to
call with this minister at the homes of some of

his people.   Of such homes among the negroes as these the white people know very little. The door is locked on both sides — on the side of the whites by their dictum of social separation; on the side of the educated negroes by their already achieved race pride and race exclusiveness.

In conclusion I am reminded of the Irishman's saying that in one respect all women are alike — in that they are all different.   My one generalization concerning the religious life of the negroes in the South is that without qualification it is impossible to generalize.

NEW TENDENCIES IN THE
OLD SOUTH

V

NEW TENDENCIES IN THE OLD SOUTH

IN most of the sermons and religious addresses I heard in the South the conception of religion seemed to be that of a preparation for a world to come rather than a mode of earthly life. The matter for chief concern seemed to be, not for the relation of the individual with his God and his fellow-men, but rather the condition of his soul after death. In respect, therefore, to religion which did not deal primarily with the affairs of a rational existence in this world, congregations seemed to be expected to suspend their reasoning power and put in its place an unquestioning credence — called faith — in the formulas, always purporting to be derived directly from the Bible, which set forth the way to attain a happy eternal des-

tiny. It would be a mistake to infer from this
that I found religion divorced from morality.
On the contrary, nowhere have I heard moral
precepts more explicitly, even dogmatically,
asserted than by Christian people of the South.
But these precepts seemed to be regarded either
as tests for ascertaining the sincerity of conversion or as rules more or less arbitrarily imposed
upon believers. Religion was considered to be
not so much motive infusing all life as one of
the departments, though to be sure the chief
department, of existence.

This view of religion may account for the
fact that I found religion easily alluded to
under all sorts of circumstances. A group of
men in a Georgia city club, their " high balls "
being all the while brought to them in rapid
succession by the waiter, were as ready to mention, and dismiss, the subject of religion as the
subject of college education or initiation into
the ancient order of " Buffaloes."

The prevalence of this view of religion makes
it easy to understand why there is so large a
proportion of church membership to the population in the South. It is much simpler to
forego the right of rationalizing religion and
keeping aloof from the Church if one is assured

that by joining the Church one need substitute unquestioning credence only in regard to a future life considerably removed from every-day affairs. In Richmond, Virginia, the Secretary of the Young Men's Christian Association, a Pennsylvanian, told me that it was almost impossible to find men who would do personal religious work. On the other hand, both from testimony and from direct evidence, I was convinced that both church attendance and church membership were natural and expected. The secretary I have just mentioned, in the same breath in which he deplored the lack of spirituality of the young men of Richmond, declared that it was "the thing" there for men to belong to the Church. Others more intimately associated with the city—one, for instance, a physician, whose conversation leaned more naturally to the race problem in its pathological aspects and to politics than to religion—told me without qualification that this was true. On the Sunday that I spent in Richmond I attended the morning service of a Baptist church. The congregation filled the pews. I was ushered to a pew toward the front, where I was shown every courtesy by the occupants. It was Communion Sunday, and as the church practiced "close

Communion," I withdrew at the end of the preaching service; but, for the first time in my life under those circumstances, I found myself in the minority. The majority of the congregation—and I do not think my judgment regarding this is at fault — remained for Communion. This experience helped me to understand why it happened that there were lying on the table in my room at the hotel two books which I had at first thought to be the forgotten possessions of a former occupant of the room, but soon discovered to be a Book of Common Prayer and a Testament and Psalms, the property of the hotel.

About this ingenuous regard for the externals of religion there is the same elusive charm that hovers over Southern hospitality. It defies analysis, but it is very persuasive. An incident told me by a Northern man describes this better than any one experience I had. With another Northerner, he was guest at the table of an old Virginia family. When the dessert had been served, the old negro serving-man brought in, on the same tray on which he had brought the dishes, a prayer-book. The hostess and mother, an elderly lady, then read a psalm, and afterward, with the whole family, knelt there at the

table and read the beautiful form of prayer pre-
scribed for use in families.   In these simple but
formal devotions the two Northern guests
joined, of course.   Then they all withdrew to
the drawing-room for their coffee.   To these
two men in their own homes this procedure
would have been embarrassing.   There it seemed
to be a part of the gracious hospitality that had
been extended to them.   And as religious observances are in the South as naturally included
in the hospitality of the home as anything else,
so, conversely, hospitality in the South is an
integral part of the church services.   In the
hotel at Richmond I was standing in front of
the church register on Sunday evening, trying
to decide which of the Presbyterian churches I
should attend, when a young man approached,
and, as I turned, offered to me, with some apology, a card of the Brotherhood of St. Andrew,
and invited me to attend Grace Episcopal
Church.   He explained that he was not accustomed to doing this sort of thing, but undertook
to act as a substitute for a friend of his.   He
had ventured to speak to me because I was looking at the bulletin of churches.   How could I help
accepting his invitation, so courteously and personally given?   At the church, as I was stand-

ing alone in the vestibule, a gentleman of military bearing entered, and, at once seeing that I was a stranger, bade me welcome as if I were a guest at his own house, and proffered me a seat. Soon afterwards I was greeted by another host; I had been welcomed to the church, now I was welcomed to the pew. They may have "hospitality committees" in the South; if they do, they count "hospitality" the genus, and "committee" the species. It is the reverse in the North, where there are committees for everything, and incidentally for welcoming strangers. Northern church hospitality is a system; Southern church hospitality is an instinct.

At Petersburg, where I spent only a part of one day, it happened that I felt more of the historic religious atmosphere than anywhere else in the South. Perhaps that was due to the sight of the ruined old Blandford Church, which stands on the hill overlooking the city, guarding the graves of Confederate dead and bearing the scars that it received while in the line of fire from the Federal troops. A ruin always suggests history. It was built before 1731, but, unlike the old Fork Church I saw near Hanover, it had long been out of use. It represented, however, the old parish which from 1650 onward for many decades was the ruling power. The Church of England in those days was supported by glebe. The vestry had rights over property and even over life. From where I stood I could see the "crater" made by the explosion of the Confederate magazine; the place where Butler's troops faced Lee's and Jackson's; and off toward the sea the place where, three generations before, Lafayette had been stationed. Every foot of ground seemed to have been harried first by British, then by Federal "invaders." And the history of religion there seemed to be of conflict, too: the Scotch Presbyterians, who were the first settlers; the more aristocratic families of the Anglican communion; the Baptists, zealous for doctrine; the Methodists, rising against the fox-hunting, carousing Episcopal parsons; the Disciples, forming a new sect in remonstrance against sectarianism; finally, Bohemians from Prague and Pilsen, who were all Roman Catholics — one ecclesiastical army after another has made of this battle-ground of two wars a spiritual battle-ground as well. Land so plowed and harrowed does not furnish much of a crop — principally " ground-peas " and doctrines. My host and guide, an intense Virginian, well

versed in local history, had not much to say of
distinctively religious conditions; what he did
say I may briefly summarize as follows: Two
old Presbyterian churches, which were built
when the women brought in their aprons the
sand for the mortar, still stand; the Episcopalian churches, which in the old days of the
glebe were under a rector and curate, are combined in a circuit under one rector; Methodists
and Baptists are numerically strong; and the
Catholics are segregated locally and racially.
In one respect this is a picture of all of the
South that I saw: a country still suffering from
the desolating effects of civil and spiritual
war.

This sectarian spirit is partly due to the
regard for externals I have referred to; for
there is bound to be disunion where there is
more allegiance to the uniform than to the
Leader; but it is also partly due to the individualism of the South. The peculiar character of Southern individualism I have not yet
been able, even measurably, to analyze. As I
saw it, however, its distinctive quality seemed
to be institutional. The personal individualism
of the New England Puritan, whose prophets
are Emerson and Thoreau, and whose types

throng the stories of Miss Wilkins and Miss
Jewett, seemed to me to be conspicuously
absent; but in its place there was an institutional individualism connoted everywhere. The
part was assumed to be greater than the whole:
in politics, the State than the Nation, and the
city than the State; in religion, Protestantism
than Christianity, and the denomination than
either. The more individual the institution,
the more did I hear of insistence on its rights.
But not an iota further did individualism go.
In the democracy of the South, which in many
respects is more distinctively American than
that of any other portion of the Union, the unit
is something larger than the individual voter.
The ordinances of secession were passed, with
but one exception, without being submitted to
the people, and this year of 1901 has seen one
Southern State establish a new Constitution, for
the express purpose of asserting the individualism of that State, without popular ratification.
In much the same way in the Protestantism of
the South, it is the liberty of the denomination
rather than that of the individual soul that is
asserted. Doctrinal dissent of any kind, of
which any denomination is sponsor, I found to
be more in evidence in the South than anywhere

else; but I do not think I met a single Southerner who openly confessed to skepticism.

When I left Richmond, the air was raw and
chill; when, the next morning, I arrived in
Charleston, the air was as balmy as the quiet
breeze of a June day in my Maine home under
the pines. Every breath I drew proved to me
that during the night I had been whisked into a
new world. And as I drove through the streets
every sight told me of an unfamiliar land.
Everything looked grizzled, weather-beaten,
ancient. The houses were low and large, with
wide, high-pillared piazzas, one above another.
The full-leaved magnolias and the tropical
palmettoes in the door-yards emphasized the
strangeness. Soon I was wandering about the
city; under the portico of old St. Philip's
Church, in the belfry of which each night there
shines a beacon to guide the sailors in the har-
bor; past the quaint old Huguenot Church, the
only one existing in America; along the South
Battery that looks out to Fort Sumter; then up
Meeting Street to St. Michael's Church. As at
St. Philip's, the sidewalk runs beneath the portico; like almost every other building in the
city, the stucco has fallen in great patches from
its walls. Beneath the pavement not only of

the churchyard walks, but also of the vestibule itself, lie the dead whose very names mean South Carolina—Rutledge, Pinckney, De Saussure. The sexton, a comparatively young man, proudly showed me the church, which for nearly a century and a half has survived in spite of British artillery and Federal cannonading, of cyclone and earthquake. More eloquent of conservatism than the old "Governor's pew," once "occupied by General Washington," or the old organ made in 1767, or the pulpit panel stolen by some one who followed the army of occupation in 1865 and some years later anonymously returned, or the service of altar plate stolen from its refuge in Columbia during the war, of which only two pieces, a flagon and a cover, were recovered, one from a New York pawnshop, the other from somewhere in Ohio, was the simple statement of the sexton that he had held his office for ten years, that his father, now dead, had been sexton for fifty years before him, that his mother, now eighty-seven, still cut the bread for Communion, and that the old bellringer who had lately died had rung the chimes for sixty-one years.

To this historic past the Huguenot Church is even a more impressive monument. Its building

is only a half-century old; but its organization
dates probably from the very year of the founding of the city.   Gradually, with the loosing of
the bond of a distinctive language, the Huguenot families became absorbed into the Episcopal which was the established church, and the
Huguenot Church grew weaker and weaker.
But with the change from the use of French to
English the church revived, and to-day it remains, the only one of its name in this land.   It
was my privilege to attend the service there
Sunday afternoon, and to join in the simple,
impressive liturgy which, unchanged almost
wholly except in tongue, preserved the form of
worship used by the Huguenots of Neuchâtel
and Valangin.   It was a still greater privilege
to know the venerable and revered pastor of the
church, Dr. Vedder, and be enriched not only
by the genial hospitality of himself and his
gracious wife, but also by his store of knowledge of the city and its life.

Much of what elsewhere is regarded as essential to human nature seems to have been
dispensed with in Charleston.   The participa-
tion of Charleston in the project of secession I
can now regard only as an act of supereroga-
tion; for, though the city is now a loyal portion

of the Union, to all intents and purposes it seems as separate from the United States as if it were an independent municipality. In no respect is this isolation shown in better light than by the contempt which the highest society of the city displays toward the plutocrat. Although at its most exclusive functions may be seen a sempstress or a street-car conductor whose family, impoverished by "the War between the States," has in no way lost its social status, the merely rich are inexorably excluded. No newspaper there would venture or care to print an account of these exclusive assemblies. The social set that provides the standard of social taste and tone for the city would not tolerate the sycophancy of the "yellow journals," or indeed journals of other hue, that devote whole columns to what rich women wear at the New York Horse Show. Charleston has a human nature of its own, in this respect so admirable that it is worthy of mention in an account of religious life in America. Paradoxical as it may sound, Charleston is thus undoubtedly typical of the "Old South." From such a human nature there naturally grows a religious conservatism, not polemical or self-assertive, as in the North, but when undisturbed affable, when controverted merely cold, like the conservatism of an English university.

In one respect, however, human nature in Charleston is like human nature in other places: ministers recuperate from Sunday by getting together and talking "shop" on Monday!— on the principle, I suppose, of *similia similibus curantur.* To this meeting I was invited. The paper read was on methods to be used in visiting the sick in hospitals. Both that and the discussion following connoted a vast deal of patient, tactful, merciful labor of love among the sick poor. When the subject of the next meeting was announced, there were a number of inquiries as to what it meant. The subject was Social Settlements! It was finally stated that the real name was College Settlement, but just what it was only one minister present seemed to know. He was the young minister of the old Circular Church — a Congregational church (the only white one in the State) founded in 1690. I had a conversation with this Congregational minister, who, though a Southerner by birth, was a Westerner by training — his speech betrayed him — and was originally a Methodist. He told me he had introduced the subject for the purpose of enlightening his brother ministers.

(To the credit of those same brother ministers, every one with whom I spoke was pleased to be enlightened, and seemed to take fraternal pride in this young minister's bustling ways.) I found that he was keenly aware of the social aspect of Christianity, and was greatly interested in workingmen, and was proud of the fact that not only had his church increased in membership in spite of a decrease in the white population of the city, but that its increase had come from the working classes.

"Do you find any opposition to this from the people of old families in your church?"

"Not exactly opposition. But one day after Communion, when some of the common people were admitted to membership, a rich lady came up to me and said, 'But remember, it is quality we want, not quantity.' That expresses their attitude."

Here is typified one of the new religious tendencies in the Old South — to accept, conservatively and with some remonstrance, it may be, the leadership of men who, though alien in training and in sentiment, are genuine and not presumptuous. The surprisingly receptive and adaptable spirit of most of the Southerners I met helped to explain to me the

tremendous recuperation of the South, both
commercial and educational, since the war, and
made deeply significant of possible results such
occasional presentations of the " social gospel "
as were given by this enthusiastic minister from
the West.

A second religious tendency in the South is
to experiment within the safe limits of evangelical theology with extraordinary religious ideas.
An illustration of this occurred to me while I
was in Charleston. It was at a meeting of people of various denominations interested in
" Anglo-Israelism " — the theory that the so-
called " lost ten tribes " of Israel are perpetu-
ated in the Anglo-Saxon peoples. On the
previous Sunday in a church I had heard a sermon in which this theory was incidentally advo-
cated. This evening the address was by a clergyman of a different denomination. The hall was
small, the audience was smaller. The voice of
the speaker, however, was suited not to the size
of the auditorium so much as to his conception
of the bigness of his subject, and that was very
big indeed. He started by saying that the
identity between the Saxon tribes and lost
Israel was indisputable, and that we should lay
aside preconceived ideas, for in a progressive

age it was unfortunate to be so conservative as to avoid this conclusion! Then, taking Abraham, his servant, and his son as types of the Father, the Holy Ghost, and Christ, he concluded that Christ must take his Bride the Church from his own kin, that is, some tribes of the Hebrew people—"otherwise these types cannot be preserved"! Promises thus given to Israel must be fulfilled by Israel; they are being fulfilled by the English-speaking people: therefore the English-speaking people are Israel. We are consequently the elect, the conquering race. Patriotism and religion are identical; supremacy of the race must be maintained; Queen Victoria and President McKinley are leaders of God's elect; all our history, all our life, is sacred. Before he closed he declared: "The very belief that Christ died for me is not more buoyant and vitalizing than this assurance that I am one of God's elect." Obviously absurd as this doctrine is, it is more reasonable than the notions that have served to sustain some new sects in the North and the West, and has evidently proved more efficacious than other and perhaps sounder beliefs in leading some people to waken to certain moral and spiritual truths of which before they had been wholly unaware. There are, moreover, three things in particular that ought to be said about this before it is judged unworthy of much consideration. The first is that although the number of Anglo-Israelites seemed small, the serious and judicial consideration their theory received from the few clergymen and the one representative layman with whom I had the opportunity of referring to the subject was impressive. (One minister, however, told me that he "preferred to take his Higher Criticism straight.") The second is that this is only one of a number of such movements, among which I had occasion more than once to note the "Holiness" doctrine as important. The third is that, like the "Holiness" doctrine, this theory of Anglo-Israelism arouses in many minds, accustomed to the idea that religion has almost exclusively to do with an intangible soul and a future heaven, the dormant sense of the sacredness of this present life; and, besides, shifts the object of their religious loyalty (at least on the human side) away from the narrow sphere of the denomination to the broader one of the race.

The two religious tendencies of the South which I have mentioned—the one to accept new leadership provided it is genuine, enthusiastic, and not presumptuous, the other to experiment within the confines of formal orthodoxy with novel, sometimes fantastic, and even preposterous religious theories and inventions — are both pronounced and extensive. Another religious tendency in the South, the third and last that I shall mention, is that away from a mechanical toward a vital theology on the one hand, and on the other hand away from a purely individualistic toward a social Christian activity on the part of Southern religious leaders themselves. This I regard as the most important and widespread of these tendencies. To my experiences which illustrate this tendency I shall devote the remainder of this chapter.

An acknowledged leader in education in the South gave me very frankly his opinion that Southern men of influence do not dare to express their thoughts as against the predominating dogmatic beliefs, not because they are unheroic, but because they know it would be useless. But gradually, for instance through the libraries into which books of the modern sort are introduced without protest, there is increasing an undercurrent of thought that is sweeping past the old dogmas. The stage of development at present he described as that of the separation between theory and practice. When I asked him as to the soundness of the hopeful spirit of the South, he was inclined to be dubious. "It is not based on the historic sense; that is wholly lacking. People here [mentioning his own State] are not like those of Virginia or the North; they are great fighters, but they don't know how to retreat; when they have to give up they are in rout. I find evidence of this among the young men in college. When they fail, they don't try for a new opening, but go home. That is why I believe that when the South wakes up to the new thought it will have to go through the stage of superficial infidelity."

Partly in confirmation of this opinion and partly to indicate the influences at work in the South which, if triumphant, will make the stage of superficial infidelity unnecessary, I quote in part a conversation with the pastor of a prominent Baptist church of Charleston.

"We are starting a church library," he told me, "containing not only Sunday-school but also general reference books, and religious books for use in studying the Bible and other religious topics. In this library are included many books that are not sound from the Baptist point of view. Such a book went into one man's family. He read it and disapproved; but, instead of making a disturbance, he sent his check for twenty-five dollars and bought the set to which the volume belonged (the set was worth about ten dollars), simply to remove them from the library. But even such conservatism is disappearing. Another distinction of this church is that there is somewhat more than the usual proportion of men."

" How do you account for that? "

"In the first place, the church is centrally located. In the second place, the pastors have always been accustomed to deal with current topics fearlessly when there was an unmistakable religious phase to them. The church has grown sixty per cent. in the ten years in which the city has lost five thousand in white population."

When it is remembered that it is difficult to speak of any current topic in the South without becoming involved in the race question,[1] to

---

[1] Unquestionably the existence of the race question in the South has had a great deal to do in inducing the churches there to avoid the ethical and social aspects of Christianity, and to lay chief emphasis upon its doctrinal and theological amplifications. Under such conditions it is only natural that ministers who find a "simple Gospel " (as they call the most abstruse speculations about the Gospel which do not happen to touch by any chance upon practical life) a much easier and safer subject to preach about than "morality " or "sociology " (as they call all treatment to-day of men's relations to one another, no matter how Christlike the motive or spirit) are quite emphatic in declaring that the Church should not concern itself with anything but the " plan of salvation."

which the Southern mind is of course extremely sensitive, this statement as to the character of the preaching and the growth of the church has special significance. Here was exemplified, in a city church, the blending of two phases of the most important tendency I noted in the South—toward a larger liberty of thinking and a greater emphasis on the Gospel in relation to the social life. How this tendency is affecting the Church in the small towns and the country regions of the South I had a good opportunity of observing in a trip I took with a Methodist presiding elder.

My companion was a man of stocky build and of a countenance that at once invited confidence. Before the train was well under way he was telling me stories of his experiences, mingled with most cheerful tales of negroes and accounts of the places through which we were passing. I found him to be a man of very open mind. Though there was no touch of radicalism in his thought, he was not unacquainted or unsympathetic with the modern movements in theology. In the midst of his breezy stories there was an occasional suggestion, all the more emphatic because entirely unconscious, of a most spontaneous spirit of

Christian self-sacrifice. I was glad to see that a man of such personality had been chosen by the Methodist Church South to be a presiding elder, a teacher of teachers, a preacher to preachers. Because I have not hesitated to record some observations of ministerial self-interest and ambition, I want to emphasize the unselfishness and the serene indifference to anything like personal advancement which I found so apparent in this man of influence in the Methodist Church. His attitude of amused contempt for the ecclesiastical place-hunter he expressed a day or so later when, as we alighted from a carriage, I took up his valise. "It is entirely too early to do that sort of thing," he said, jokingly, "even if you do want a transfer from Maine to South Carolina; ministers don't treat the presiding elder in that fashion until about Conference time, when the new appointments are to be made. Until then the presiding elders all carry their own valises."

His appreciation of the sociological aspect of church work may be suggested by an incident he related. Part of his district includes the mill region. He chose two of the most active and promising young men under his charge to work there among the operatives. The editor of a religious paper remonstrated with him. "What do you mean," he asked, "by putting such men as those *down there?*" "I want just such men as those to study the question of industrial conditions." In spite of the editor's remark, "It will never do; they won't stay," it did do and they stayed.

We got off the train at a small factory town, and were welcomed by the Methodist minister and the superintendent of the mills. We were made the minister's guests. Although he was a Southerner born and bred, he had something of the Western eagerness for self-development and Northern readiness "either to tell or to hear some new thing." As we sat before the open fire he turned the conversation irresistibly to modern religious books. The fact that I was from the North aroused all his appetite for information; and instead of my questioning him I found myself put to it to answer his questions as to the most recent books on such subjects as the Hebrew Prophets, Christianity and Sociology, Evolution, and the "New Theology." It came out in the course of the evening that, in lieu of having at hand popular works on the subject of evolution and religion, he had turned to and written and published a book on the subject himself.

At the meeting in the church that evening the small audience comprised twice as many men as women. This was partly explained by the fact that a Ladies' Bible Class was in session at the same time. The service, conducted by my hospitable guide, was not extraordinary in any way; it was simply helpful. The church, I was told, was made up largely of mill operatives. The superintendent of the mill, a Northern man now a thorough and enthusiastic convert to the South, a man too of whose helpful, unostentatious friendship for the poor and friendless I heard many accounts, contributed to the democratic atmosphere of the church, and, so far as I could see, did not assume to be even *primus inter pares*.

The next day the presiding elder and I drove in a buggy through three mill districts, past a ramshackle little group of houses occupied by negroes, which boasted of two churches, one of which bore on its steeple the only sign of paint I saw in the whole settlement, then over a dull, dreary stretch of land where negroes were plowing with mules, until we reached a

little meeting-house under the edge of the
"piny woods." That we were half an hour
late seemed to disturb none of the dozen or fifteen that were assembled. At the service, which
was not quarterly meeting as expected because
of the absence of certain laymen, the presiding
elder again spoke simply but without the sign
of intellectual alertness that sparkled in his conversation. At the close of service we were
made the guests of a clergyman, formerly a
Methodist preacher but now superannuated on
account of nervous ill health. Another guest
was the local preacher in charge of this and one
or two other churches. He took me for a drive
about the country in the afternoon. He proved
to be open-minded, like his ecclesiastical supe-
riors, and well aware of the problems presented
by the gradually decreasing population, though
by no means certain as to the solution of them.
As we talked over the subject of his sermon for
the morrow, on the text "Behold the Lamb of
God!" he responded eagerly to the conclusion
which was developed in the course of our conversation, that the sacrifice of Christ was the
consequence not of an arbitrary fiat but of a
universal law which throughout all life makes
the redeemer the chief sufferer in the process of

redemption. Our host, though exhausted by a fight with a forest fire which he had kept a secret from us until he had gotten it under control, was not only as suave and delightful as he would have been under circumstances of ease and leisure, but, like the others of this exceedingly interesting group of ministers, most broad in his intellectual sympathies.

The next day, Sunday, I went with the family to the services. During Sunday-school I purposely remained outside to get a chance to talk with the farmers. I am afraid I kept them from the session of the school, and for recompense I found little to enlighten me on their view of religious conditions. One of the replies I received is, however, worth recording. We had been discussing the condition of the outward observance of religion in that country community. Remembering the frequency with which I had noticed in the rural town in Maine where I live the farmers getting in their hay or hauling the corn to the canning-factory on Sunday, I inquired whether men there in South Carolina worked on Sunday more now than formerly. One of the men who had spoken discouragingly of the regard for Sunday looked up surprised at my question and rather puzzled, and replied, " No one ever does farm work on Sunday; people here are careless, but they are not sacrilegious."

The quarterly meeting followed the morning service. In the administration of the Communion at the close of this meeting, I, though not a Methodist, was asked to participate. Then, after a necessarily hurried luncheon, we drove back to the factory town, where quarterly meeting again was held. At each occasion the presiding elder made an address similar in spirit to the preceding addresses. One might attend church services in the South for a considerable period without discovering any intellectual spontaneity—either of origination or of receptivity—among the ministers ; but one could scarcely fail to see signs of such intellectual spontaneity in almost any minister through personal conversation. This, at least, was indicated not only by my experience on the occasion I have just described, but also throughout my whole Southern trip. Whatever ferment may be occasioned by the leaven of modern theological thought and social consciousness in the church life of the South is beneath the surface. Probably on that very account it is more widespread, and as a result, possibly, the country churches of the South will not be the last to be affected by larger religious conceptions.

In a previous chapter I have already referred to the heroic and successful work of Mr. George Williams Walker, a thorough Southerner, in carrying on, in Augusta, Georgia, a Southern Methodist institute for negroes. I cannot close this chapter on new religious tendencies, intellectual and social, without referring to another heroic work done in the same city. When I was told of the work being done by the clergyman of an Episcopal church in the mill district, I called upon him at his house. He cordially assented to my suggestion that I accompany him on his pastoral calls. In accordance with this plan we started out on bicycles for a tour of the district. There are a number of cotton-mills along the canal just outside of the city limits. The houses of the employees form a settlement on the low land bordering this canal. The first house we entered (consisting of two rooms and a kitchen) was occupied by a widow and her eight children. The family was supported by the earnings of the three oldest daughters, which amounted to about fifty cents apiece each day

they could work. In this single household
during the past winter there had been several
cases of chickenpox and of measles, at least
one case of malarial fever, nine cases of grippe,
and three cases of typhoid fever, due chiefly to
the unsanitary environment of the company's
house which they had occupied. The clergyman took from his medicine-case, which he told
me he always carried with him, some mild
remedy for one of the little girls who was still
sick. The woman at whose house we next
stopped was in more comfortable circumstances
than most of her neighbors, for her husband
was a policeman. She was a woman of evident intelligence and force of character, though
she could neither read nor write. So from
house to house we went; sickness, destitution,
misery, were not the exception, but the rule;
the wretchedness of congested population was
combined with the desolation of illiteracy and
vacant minds. To the other sources of woe
was added the prevailing custom of the em-
ployment of children. How young? "Oh, I
don't know," was one pitiful answer; "power-
ful little bits of children." In one household
we visited a little boy had recently died. He
had not lived to be ten years old, and he had

worked in the factory ever since he had come from the country, a year and a half before. Most of the families were from the country— mainly from " Car'lina." The reasons given for leaving their rural homes were widely various: " because we lost our 'plantation' "; " because my wife was lonely "; " because the darkies came in." Various, too, was the testimony as to the result: some declared they had improved their conditions; others that they had ruined what good fortune they had had. At the best they were hopeless. Most of them confessed that they had abandoned the church-going habits of their country life. Being Protestants, their illiteracy made the personal devotional life among them difficult and rare, since they had recourse to neither priest nor book. Out of this population of "poor white" mill hands this clergyman had built up a church, in spite of the fact that they were naturally non-Episcopalian. In addition he was enabled to raise money to build a parish house, which at the time of my visit was to contain a small assembly-room for lectures and entertainments, a library, a reading-room, and a room for a caretaker. He put special value upon the proposed lectures and entertainments, because they

would provide for the great proportion of the
population a source of relaxation and instruction which, because of their illiteracy, they could
not get through books or periodicals. Besides
this he had raised during the past year a sum
equal to his own salary to be used in relief of
distress. One novel method he used in raising
this sum consisted in providing a special train
to run out of the city to a point where an
eclipse of the sun could be easily viewed. By
making arrangements with the railroad company, he managed to clear a considerable profit.
This charitable fund he so expended that it
became a strong influence for the independence
of the beneficiaries. In some instances it was
used as loans; in most other cases for purchase
of supplies. As a consequence every family
that was helped received aid in a constantly
diminishing quantity.

As a slight digression, I quote here what was
more than once told me, not only in Georgia,
but also in South Carolina (especially in Charleston), that the reason the Episcopalian clergymen in the South do not coöperate with other
ministers is not on High Church grounds (for
the Episcopal Church is predominantly Low
Church in the South), but because of social dis-

tinctions. This makes apposite a story that was told me of a lady newly come to live in a city of Virginia. She was asked what church she attended. "Oh," she replied, "in doctrine I'm a Presbyterian, but *socially* I'm an Episcopalian." From this feeling, of course, the minister whose work I am describing would suffer only indirectly.

It was not from this clergyman that I learned that he had practically no real assistance from the strong churches of the city — apart from financial contributions. That I learned from other sources; and it was corroborated by the clergyman himself, only reluctantly, and with explanations that did credit to his charitableness. At the Young Men's Christian Association I was told that in an address before the Association he had spoken on labor questions, and had thus not found favor with some of the "conservative people of Augusta." That he had found favor with some other people, whose favor I should value more highly, I surmised by the cordial and admiring response the mention of his name called forth as I was chatting with a street-car conductor.

This may seem to be a gloomy picture. One side of it is; but not the other side, which shows a man of fine fiber, both in mind and taste, single-handed bringing to a forlorn and destitute people, stricken with ignorance and disease, the gospel not only of words but of deed, the good news of health, knowledge, comfort, recreation, comradeship. If that is gloomy, so is the Parable of the Good Samaritan.

NEW ORLEANS

VI

NEW ORLEANS

THERE is a game — the psychologists call it an experiment — which may be named for short Redintegration. The psychologist calls out a word and you reply with another word expressing a related idea, and, lo! the "structure of your soul" is revealed. Suppose the word is "subject." If you answer "cadaver," you are proved to be a medical student; if "predicate," then you are certainly a student or teacher of grammar; but if "text," then you are without doubt a minister. In the same way, if "New Orleans" be suggested, the New England housewife will think "molasses"; the Grand Army veteran will think "Butler"; perhaps somebody inclined to the legendary will be naïve enough to say "spoons!" But most of us will be apt to think "Creole." So at least it was with me. As soon as I decided to go to New Orleans it was the old French Catholic atmosphere that I expected to breathe. That is why, as soon as I reached the city, I started off toward the French quarter across Canal Street. The width of this great dividing street, with its broad strip in the center reserved for the several electric car tracks, accentuated the lowness of the buildings on either hand. Growing by the side of these tracks was a four-leafed clover, which I picked and sent to my wife, not only as a sign of summer in the time when snow is deepest in Maine, but also as a symbol of the leisureliness of Southern life. A city in whose central thoroughfare a four-leafed clover can flourish must be characterized by a repose not distinctively American. And again I said to myself " Creole."

A narrower street in the French quarter soon led me between two high walls. I turned to the left and went through a gate. I found myself in what seemed to be a miniature city of brick, stucco, and marble. Down the center ran a street, grass-grown, deserted. The buildings on either side looked like dwarf temples, the highest towering several feet above my head. It seemed as if some pygmean race had here

built and then abandoned a sacred city. It was
the old St. Louis Cemetery. The temples were
tombs. On their fronts were inscribed, in most
cases in French, the names of the dead. Here
and there hung the faded remnants of wreaths
and bunches of flowers.

Many of the tombs, so the inscriptions indicated, were built and maintained by associations
formed for the purpose of providing entomb-
ment for their members. Here certainly was a
contrast to that individualism evident among
other white people in the South. In this sign of
the social instinct, strong even in death, there
was a reminder once more of that insistent word
" Creole."

On Sunday morning I went to high mass at
the French Cathedral of St. Louis. On my way
there I noticed tacked on the trees printed slips
of paper with borders in black. They were
announcements — with few exceptions they
were in French—of the death of various individuals. On each of these there was a list of
families whose attention was called to that
special obituary notice. Pride of lineage, the
social instinct, and religion were all blended on
these bits of paper.

On I went through the narrow streets where

children played in the doorways and on the pavement, until I came out at Jackson Square. There stood the old Cathedral looking out toward the levees. I entered, and at the entrance to the gallery paid five cents to the doorkeeper. I found that I was on the side over the pulpit. So I descended, crossed over, paid another coin, and entered the gallery on the other side. To a non-Catholic, service in every Catholic church seems much the same. In each there is the same atmosphere of sanctity and mystery; the same unstudied reverence in the worshipers, that makes the Puritan wonder at the stiffness of his own knees; the same vestments and lights that somehow seem regal and courtly, as well as religious and almost histrionic; the same indefinable influence — is it of the music? — that makes religion seem not something merely intellectual, as does the ultra-Protestant "meeting," nor something celestially pure, as does the Anglican liturgy, but something intensely human, terrestrial, dramatic; the same wail in the Kyrie Eleïson; the same militant confidence in the Credo; the same sudden, awesome, shuddering silence at the sound of the bell; the same sudden awakening to the normal healthfulness and buoyancy of life upon egress to the

open air and sunlight. Perhaps in this uniformity of service lies one of the secrets of the
power of the Roman Catholic Church; for it
seems as if the Catholic worshipers, especially
in this land where education, politics, and even
languages and races are in constant flux and
conflict, must be impressed everywhere with
the unity of his unaltered and, outwardly at
least, unalterable Church. It was impossible
for me at least to differentiate the religious
characteristics of the Catholic services of such
widely differing cities, for instance, as Baltimore, New Orleans, and Little Rock. The
one contrast, of course — and that chiefly an
external one — was in the language used for
the gospel, epistle, and sermon, which in New
Orleans was French. There was, however, a
difference in congregations. In Baltimore the
people at the service showed by their clothes
and carriage that they were, most of them,
wealthy; in Little Rock they were distinctly
from the humbler ranks — most of them might
have been servants. Here in the Cathedral at
New Orleans the congregation seemed much
less homogeneous. In an obscure gallery near
the altar were a number of nuns. In the body
of the church the people seemed to represent

a variety of the grades of life. There was, however, no display of wealth. On the other hand, there was an indefinable trace of aristocracy in the faces and bearing of some of the people. Many of the women wore deep mourning. A number of negroes were present, seated on benches along the walls. A man in some sort of uniform with epaulets was moving about the church showing people to their seats and inspiring the doorkeepers with zeal for keeping people quiet; he was apparently the verger. When the sermon was about to begin, many negroes on the side aisle pressed up near the pulpit. One old lame black man hobbled forward with the rest and stood throughout the sermon, leaning on his cane and looking intently up into the preacher's face. When the sermon was finished, they all returned to their places for the rest of the service.

As the congregation passed out I went to find Père Mignot, to whom I had a letter of introduction. Up the narrow little alley beside the cathedral I went, and knocked at the door to which I was directed. I found him very busy. He was short and stout — the cassock he wore extended to his feet; a beard, such as the members of his order are entitled to wear, long and

gray, gave to his round, happy face a quality of
fatherliness; and his eyes had a benignant light
that invited confidence. When, a few days
later, I called on him again, he was freer to
talk and walk with me. He took me upstairs
to where hung the valued portraits of the first
Bishop, and the first Pastor, and the Founder
of the Parish of New Orleans. Père Mignot's
ecclesiastical dress seemed to link him in time
with these dignitaries of the past, and his
French, which he exchanged for broken English
as he talked with me, seemed to place him in
the Old World. I felt as if I were crudely
modern — out of place and time. He said he
would show me the Convent of the Holy Family,
a convent for colored nuns. We had been talking about the French and Spanish negro Catholics, and as we went along he told me that some
of these were leaving the Catholic Church.
"They find the Church too strict," he said,
"and they go off to the Baptists and others
where they can dance and shout. Some of
them leave because they are sensitive about
being with white people in church, and they become Protestant so they can go to a church
where all are of one color."

I asked him if the Catholic Church in New

Orleans was giving the negroes industrial training in the schools — and explained what I
meant by referring to Booker Washington.
Père Mignot had not heard about Booker Washington. It was evident that, beyond the usual
instruction in sewing and cooking, and some
minor occupations like the putting together of
artificial flowers, as later I observed, he knew of
no industrial education in the Catholic schools.
At the Convent of the Holy Family, which
Père Mignot told me was first established over
fifty years ago for free negroes, the placid faces
of the colored nuns in their hoods of black and
white, and their quiet, mellifluous voices, were
like a benediction. The next day Père Mignot
accompanied me to the school taught by the
Sisters of the Sacred Heart. I expect never to
be confronted with a stronger argument for
parochial schools than that given by the bright-
ening faces of the children at the sight of his
genial, fatherly presence, their eagerness for his
blessing, and their glad, quiet, ingenuous devoutness as they knelt to receive that blessing
before his departure. I felt better for kneeling
with those Creole children in their school-room.

Of very different type was a young Creole
priest whom I had the pleasure of meeting. I

first saw him in his room in the house adjoining his church. He might well have sat, or rather stood, for a portrait of Giuseppe Caponsacchi; and when he spoke, his seemed to be "the steadfast eye and quiet word o' the Canon of the Pieve!" Only it was not in Italian but in the soft *legato* English of the Creole that he spoke. In his conversation, as in his face, there glowed the devotional mysticism that suggests Faber, and Thomas à Kempis, and Bernard of Clairvaux. He asked me to be seated near where stood a prie-dieu over which hung a crucifix.

"Some Protestants have strange ideas of the Catholic religion," he said in the course of his conversation. He told me thereupon that once a young Protestant woman had asked him how Catholics defended their worship of the Holy Virgin; and he explained that they did not worship the Mother of Jesus as they worshiped God. "There on my desk stand two pictures: one is 'of my mother," he said, "the other is of the Blessed Virgin. I adore my mother"— he had a way of using English words with a French significance — "and I adore the Blessed Virgin. I can go to my mother and confide in her and get help; so I believe I can go to the Mother of Christ and get help.

"Here in New Orleans" — I cannot quote his exact words — "there are three old Latin elements among the population: the French, the Spaniards, and the Italians. You call all Italians 'Dagos'; but really the Dagos are simply the Sicilians. Now, my work is chiefly among the French."

"Are they good Catholics?" I asked.

"Yes," he answered; "but with them religion is very much a matter of routine."

With somewhat of a digression, I quoted what some Catholic workingmen had said to me.

"Catholic workingmen do not believe all they say against the Church. When sickness comes, or death, they say then what they believe; though sometimes a man on his death-bed, if others are present, will say to the priest that he will see him, not as a priest, but as a friend. One priest, who was pastor for thirty-six years, said that in all that time only six or seven resisted him at the point of death."

"What happens if they get well?"

"Habitually they practice religion. But" — with a smile — "they go off fishing Saturday nights and do not return till Monday, and they get out of the way of going to mass." There was a tone of pity in his voice as he said this; as if he sympathized with men who had temptations to which he, as a priest, could not by circumstance and temperament be liable. "Catholics, especially in America, have a great deal of reverence for the Church and for the priest. A priest who came from France to visit this country told me he was astounded at the respect, indeed friendship, shown to priests by the people. Even in New York as he walked along the streets many people, strangers, would touch their hats as they met him. So in the hotels and even in railroad trains. This would not be so in France. In New Orleans it is even more than this — it is friendliness. In France, and among the old French people here who have been educated in France, it is always '*monsieur l'abbé*,' but among the Creoles it is always '*père*.'

"In the religion of the Creoles there is something more than this reverence for the Church. It is the — the — how do you say it? — *respect humain*."

"Deference for public opinion?" I suggested. I could think of nothing better than this clumsy English phrase.

"Something like that," he said hesitatingly.

"You hardly know what it is; it doesn't exist so much among the English; it is a Latin trait. A great deal of religion among the Creoles is due to that. It is that which makes their religion seem like routine."

I think I know what he meant: the sense of honor, as Brownell in his "French Traits" points out—a kind of conformity to the enlightened opinion of the race, substituted for conscience as the guide of conduct. This, it may be inferred, saves the Creoles, as it does the French, from fanaticism — though not necessarily from intolerance — for the fanatic is one who tries to extend the sovereignty of his conscience beyond the bounds of his individual conduct, its rightful domain, to the conduct of others. On the other hand, even the fanatic is not always free from subservience to popular opinion; and I remarked that even in New England this *respect humain* sometimes causes people to act more in accordance with what other people think than in accordance with what they are sure is right.

"It is too much that," said the *abbé*, simply.

He admitted regretfully that the Creoles as a distinctive people are dying out. The Creole children, he told me, were mingling with chil-

dren on the other side of the city; they were
learning a smattering of English and losing
some of their French. As a consequence, he
said, there were some young people who really
knew no language. Whether in the process
they were losing their religion he did not, and
I suppose could not, say.

There was no sign of religious decadence,
at any rate, at the Benediction of the Most
Blessed Sacrament, which I attended the next
evening. It is true it was in Lent; but it was a
Thursday — not a Sunday — evening. I arrived
some time before the service began. By the
kindness of the priest I was given a seat on one
side near the altar, where chairs were placed
facing across the church, in what I should call
the chancel. In order to reach the seats on the
side where I sat the people had to pass around
behind the altar. Each man — there were no
women in this part of the church, I think — as
he approached the altar made a genuflection.
Before the service began every seat, so far as I
could see, was taken. A somber tone was given
to the congregation by the prevalence of black
in the gowns of the women. A sense of so-
lemnity pervaded the whole church. The sensitive type of countenance predominated in old

and young. Plain folk they were, yet bearing
the marks of gentility. Most of them must
have come from good homes. There were not
lacking those who bore evidence of living by
the labor of their hands. The old man who
knelt next to me was callous of hand, rough of
dress, rugged of feature. But distinctions, of
which at most there was but little sign, seemed
lost in the feeling of common dependence upon
the God whose presence they felt in the Sacrament which the priest took out from the altar
and held up in the sight of them all. And as
the choir sang the O Salutaris and the altar-boy
swung the censer so that the smoke of the
incense floated out over the kneeling people,
through every possible physical avenue to the
soul, supplanting all distractions, came the one
appeal to heed and worship a God revealed in
sacrifice. And when the sermon was preached
and the service ended and the people had all
left the church, at least one Protestant was
wondering whether these Creoles, even if their
religion was routine, and even if they were not
well convinced that God is in all life and may
be worshiped in all places and times, were not
in a better way than many who are more rational
and more conscience-driven, and yet who, intel-

lectually assenting to God's presence, never with the heart or head acknowledge it, and who never bend the knee even to Baal.

Still, however picturesque and interesting the Creoles are, they are very far from comprising all of New Orleans. Indeed, across Canal Street from the French quarter, so distinctively Roman Catholic, there is a life as distinctively Protestant. Somebody had said to me, " The farther South you go the more Southern you will find it"; and so I did find it in some of my experiences in New Orleans. Indeed, it ought not to have been surprising to meet there people who had reacted to the furthest extreme against the Latin sense of morality and religion. In that city, where theaters are open Sunday evening, I heard views concerning the observance of Sunday expressed which were not less than Sabbatarian. It was in New Orleans that I heard a prostitute confess that she went regularly to mass, though she indignantly and with convincing sincerity denied that she went there to ply her trade. On the other hand, it was also in New Orleans that I heard horror expressed that a clergyman should go to the opera during Lent. To this Protestant element belong those who even to-day are

living in the memories of the Confederacy, with
whom it is as impossible for a Northerner to
discuss the negro problem as it is for a Southerner to discuss it with an unreconstructed
Bostonian; who also, to their high credit it
should be said, are most keenly afraid of the
spirit of commercialism that may possibly follow the industrial rejuvenation of the South—
the commercial spirit that tempts churches to
pride themselves on the wealth of their congregations, and universities to measure their value
by the amount of their endowments; that
preaches the "Gospel of the Million Dollars."
If there was one moral trait emphatic in these
ultra-Southern Protestants, it was their wholesome hatred of smug holiness.

Some of the Protestants in New Orleans
whose acquaintance it was a delight to make
were Episcopalians. There were two matters
in which I think they were generally agreed:
first, that they had had more effect upon the
Catholics than the Catholics had had upon
them — and in this I am convinced that they
particularized a general truth concerning the
relation between Catholics and Protestants
throughout the country; second, that, notwith-
standing this fact, the presence of a large and

influential Catholic population in the city had made impossible any considerable ritualism or even High Church feeling among the Episcopalians, the inference being that the people who found the undiluted article available had no taste for that article diluted.

Influential both in point of numbers and by strength of character, the Presbyterians form another important body among the Protestants; and of them the acknowledged leader in New Orleans, and virtually in great measure throughout the South, is Dr. Benjamin Morgan Palmer.[1] Even before I reached New Orleans I heard many tributes to the magnetism of his personality, to the effectiveness of his doctrinal leadership, and to his human interest in the race problem; then, in New Orleans itself, again and again from men of most widely various points of view, I heard him spoken of with admiring veneration. If the one sermon I heard him preach was typical of his eloquence—and I was informed by my companion at the church that it was—his power on an audience lay, not in fervent, glowing rhetoric, often characteristic of Southern preachers, but rather in forceful, perspicuous statement which

[1] Since this chapter was written the death of this venerable minister, resulting from a street-car accident, has caused widespread personal grief.

goes from premise to conclusion with unswerv-
ing logic, reinforced by a remarkably incisive
personal vigor. The whole structure of his
thought was theological. As an illustration I
venture to state in brief the process of thought
in a portion of his sermon. In speaking of
faith, he said that the question is sometimes
raised, How can a race be saved by a single
act of faith? For an answer he took his congregation to the "foot of that tree where the
tempter brought up the issue of the veracity of
God"; there God based his promise of redemption upon the condition that man should retract
his charge against God and simply believe; this
means the withdrawal of self-assertion. It is
the same self-assertiveness that characterized
our first parents which keeps men out of the
Church to-day. "God says, 'You must be
saved *my* way, not your way; accept the substitute I offer, or die in your sins. You *must*
be saved by grace,'" otherwise men cannot be
saved at all. This theological structure had
for its foundation the historicity of that scene
in the Garden of Eden; without it the structure apparently would fall to the ground. And
yet I think the real force of the sermon was
due rather to the preacher's knowledge of hu-

man nature and of the moral inflexibility of the character of God than to skill of sermon construction or even to the mechanical exactitude of doctrinal statement. In this evening congregation, which was not large, the men outnumbered the women in the proportion of three to two.

When, the next day, I called upon Dr. Palmer, the secret of his power over not only a whole city but over a large portion of the South revealed itself as it did not in the pulpit. The fine dignity, the warmth and courtesy of his manner, the youthful vigor of his eighty years and more, and his overflow of sympathy for all things human, characterized everything that he said. The contrast between the great wealth and the mean poverty that exist side by side even in newly settled America seemed to him to be the alarming factor in the industrial situation. He expressed a very personal interest in the movements of the workingmen. Proud as he was of his connection with the Confederacy, he was even prouder of being a loyal citizen of the Union; as he expressed it, he was " an American from top to toe." He was enthusiastically interested in the vast agitation of China, and expressed joyfully his satisfaction at the triumph of our country's diplomacy there. He was sanely hopeful regarding the solution of the negro problem. Relief of the poor by organized effort, cure of the sick by hospitals and dispensaries, education of children by schools and kindergartens, have no more interested sympathizer than Dr. Palmer. But all this interest on his own part, all this effort on the part of others, he defined to me as being merely "humanitarian." When I asked him what the Presbyterian Church was doing in all this, he replied: "You know we believe that this is not a part of the Church's business. It is right for Christian people to organize charitable societies; but the duty of the Church is limited to doing the Lord's work in the Lord's way." In brief, it was his belief that the Church should devote itself exclusively to proclaiming the Gospel, or rather a plan of salvation; and that the Church would not be doing the Lord's work in the Lord's way by mingling organically with the organic life of workingmen, or by undertaking as an institution to relieve sickness, poverty, or ignorance. I wondered, as I ended my interview, whether I had not discovered why, on the one hand, I had heard such praise of the man, and, on the other, none whatever of his church.

On the same square with the Presbyterian church to which I have referred was a building devoted to a very different conception of Christianity. One rainy afternoon on a week-day as I passed this church with its doors grimly shut and with a chain and padlock on the gate, unmistakably keeping people out, I noticed this other building; for a large sign announced that it was a lodging-house and that it belonged to the Salvation Army. There was no shelter for me even under the eaves of the church, but I knew that, stranger though I was, I should be welcome at the lodging-house. So I entered. The "ensign" in charge, Mr. Scott, showed me the building, from the dormitory rooms at the top to the baths and disinfecting-rooms at the bottom. The cleanliness and order were conspicuous. Like his house, Ensign Scott was manifestly clean clear through; and he had a sensible, genuine way of speech. Fear he did not seem to know in any form, and work he seemed to covet. On the use of philanthropy in religious work his testimony was explicit. He told me he had engaged in both the " spiritual " and the " social " work of the Army — to quote the terms which the " Salvationists " use to distinguish the work done by means of preaching, singing, prayer, and personal conversation for

the making of converts from the work in relief
of all kinds of destitution — and without hesitation he asserted that he had had more success
in reaching men religiously in the "social"
work than in the "spiritual"; and explained
how right there in that lodging-house he had
opportunities of presenting Christ to men in a
very practical way; how also he could keep a
guiding as well as a protecting hand on the
untried confessor, and how he could set the
new disciple to work for his Master. Before I
went out again into the rain I sat down in the
reading-room and fell into conversation with a
man who had drifted over Nicaragua, Mexico,
California, Arizona, and I know not where else.
He represented a floating population which find
in New Orleans a convenient gathering-place
between the South and Central American
countries and the radiating territory of the
United States. For religious influence the
position of this modest Salvation Army lodging-
house was strategic.

One church, at any rate, which through the
efforts of its Northern rector has come to recognize its own strategic position, is making religion real for this floating population by the
homely means of a wood-yard. As the result

of its success it has established a lodging-house, the superintendent of which was himself one of these floaters who had come to the wood-yard for work. Besides aiding these men from South America, this church is doing good by such simple means to two other classes: the "hoboes," who have no future and want none, and men who are temporarily out of work. Through the superintendent, the rector, Mr. Warner, has been able to come in contact with these three classes of men and know their needs. He told me that from his experience he had come to believe that the South was virgin soil for all kinds of "institutional work" (as the phrase is). He had devoted his energy to this kind partly because he had found it more difficult to approach the organized laborers on account of the selfishness of their organizations.

For this conclusion I could find good reasons out of my own experience. The old organization of the Knights of Labor was to this extent unselfish, that in any labor difficulty a committee of workmen might be made up of men from various trades, and thus the sense of brotherhood was fostered. But in the present dominant organization, the Federation of Labor, the autonomy of the various trades unions tends to selfishness. This change in the spirit of organized labor was concretely described to me by a New Orleans minister who had been a member of the Knights of Labor, but who now, under the present conditions, had encountered a new obstacle. In fairness I add that one man who had been a member of both the Knights and the Federation expressed his opinion that the former were just as selfish as the latter, though he added that his opinion might be grounded on his own individual experience, which in the case of the older organization had been exceptionally bitter.

Of the wage-earners whom I have encountered in the course of my trip those in New Orleans seemed to be, nominally at least, the most closely connected with the Church. One of these, a recognized leader of the laboring men of the city, described a great many others besides himself when he said to me, "I'm a Catholic by trade, but I don't follow my profession very closely."

My conversation with this labor leader was as full of constructive suggestion as any I have had.

"The workingman goes to church, and pays a nickel," he said, "and then he hears the priest preach a sermon on 'bear your cross,' and he decides that it isn't worth a nickel. But, just the same, the Church could be the greatest power for educating and uplifting the working-men. Employers are never against organized labor when they understand it to be simply self-defense. Now the Church, without compromising itself in preaching destruction of property, could help labor by making employers understand it."

When he mentioned self-defense, I asked him whether he thought that the change in the nature of labor organization had not increased the spirit of selfishness.

"I had not thought of that," he admitted; "perhaps so. This is something the preachers could preach against and help about, if they wanted to."

As our conversation turned to the relation of organized labor to strikes he spoke very dispassionately, and though he had himself been prominent in one of the great strikes, he considered them to be an evil to be avoided, and believed in organized labor to that end. Then, speaking of the need of moral instruction, he continued:

"If only the pulpit would take this up and

educate the workingman!— for now employers
are afraid to have their workmen organized because they are ignorant. The workingmen
could be educated and the employers could be
informed by the Church. If any prominent
divine would take this up, I'd go through the
city as a missioner with him. The South presents a better chance for the churches than the
North in this respect, because the workingmen
are not so far alienated here as there; and that
is mainly due to the fact that there are not so
many foreigners among the workingmen of the
South. There is no reason why capitalist and
laborer should not get together; after all, it is
the hog idea that keeps them apart; and that is
one great thing the Church can do — it can root
out that idea. The Church without any doubt
has a far better chance to educate both the
workingmen and the employers than any other
organization. For instance, when Debs was
here to address an open meeting of workingmen,
as a matter of fact there were as many employers present as workingmen. Now of course
that was a good thing, but Debs represented
only one side. Now, if there had been a priest
or preacher standing there speaking on behalf of
good feeling, it would have been far more effec-

tive; because the Church isn't supposed to stand for either the workingman or the employer. I believe in religion. I don't know what we should do without it."

Another Catholic workingman said to me, significantly, "The best Catholics are the best workmen." In that phrase he expressed concretely one of the tests to which religion of every form was subjected by all sorts of men whom I fell in with in the course of my trip. The fruit by which they knew the religion they admired was not peace of mind but good works.

It was a matter of regret to me that I saw so little of the Jews of New Orleans, who form a distinguished and influential body in the population of the city. The slight glimpse I did have made keener my regret that I could not see more. My impression can perhaps be best given by an anecdote which a Jewish gentleman of especially fine fiber and spiritual character told me. He said that a Yankee, in the course of a conversation with him, made frequent use of the expressions " Christian forbearance " and " Christian charity." After a while this Jewish gentleman amusingly protested with the question, " That is very well, my friend, but how about *Jewish* charity and *Jewish* forbearance?"

The Yankee stopped suddenly, as if struck by a new idea, and was silent. The next day, however, he called on the Jew, and, taking his hand, said simply, "My Christian friend!"

When I left New Orleans, I carried with me the mental picture of a city very different from that which my expectant imagination had painted before I had arrived. Instead of a quaint replica of an old French town, I had seen a marvelously interesting cosmopolitan city. And as I later recalled my experiences in New Orleans, the word " Creole " actually did not again suggest itself until I began to write this record of my visit there.

THE EDGE OF THE SOUTHWEST

VII

THE EDGE OF THE SOUTHWEST

IT was in a slow accommodation train running from Memphis to Little Rock. Many times during the long morning the train was emptied and filled again with country people and traveling salesmen. Mile after mile we rumbled past long stretches of swamp-land, covered with its charred forest of spindling trees burnt to save the labor of felling, and its monotonous string of lonely, dissolute little hovels, where lazy family groups of negroes lolled and stared. Under some circumstances even people cease to be interesting; and I was heartily glad when the tedium was broken by a change of cars. I found myself crowded with a number of " drummers " in the compartment of one of the rear passenger coaches. Strewed over the floor of the car were valises and sample-cases in confusion. The conversation among the men was mainly of the various "houses" they "represented." Finally one of the "drummers" opened his valise, pulled out a bottle of whisky, and handed it about to his brothers in trade. His manner was that of a general who was summoning his forces preliminary to making his *coup de main*.

"Gentlemen," said he, "I have here the best-selling article I ever handled."

Out of the confused pile of baggage he extricated a small leather case. He pressed a spring, and the case lay open on his knees. "This is the greatest panoramic chart of Biblical history ever made. Here are some cards describing it. Keep them." He had the undivided attention of the whole group. "In the center space you will see the illustrations of Bible scenes; in the left-hand space the Scripture text giving in inspired language the statement of the historical facts. In the right-hand space appear the subjects, with the dates accurately noted. Here, for instance, is the picture of Creation, modeled closely after the Biblical language, so that we can know just how it looked — Scripture texts from Genesis on the left, date on the right. Insert this adjustable crank, and you have the next scene — Adam and Eve in the Garden of Eden — Scripture text on the left, date on the right. A child can manage it and understand it; at the same time it is instructive to the most learned Biblical scholars. Look at these indorsements from the most eminent divines and theological professors of all denominations. Nothing like it. I make a hundred and fifty dollars a month with it right here in Arkansas; I ask nothing better."

"It is certainly the best device I ever saw for making Bible study easy," remarked a rather flashily dressed member of the brotherhood.

"Why, gentlemen," declared the man with the Bible chart and the whisky, "I am ready to say that I have been a student of the Bible all my life; but I never learned so much about Bible history as I have since I have been selling this wonderful illustrated panoramic chart, the most remarkable work ever published in the interest of religion."

This incident could not have happened in the North, nor in the extreme South. In the North that sort of religious publication would not have been so commercially profitable, and, besides, no Northern man would have dared to assume such sympathy on the part of a chance group of men in a railroad train. On the other hand, in the extreme South, though the religious conceptions of this man of Arkansas might have been congenial, his aggressiveness would have been entirely out of place.

To many readers the incident I have related of the man in the train may seem to be exaggerated, or at least extreme. It was, however, a striking confirmation of what was told me by the Secretary of the Young Men's Christian Association in one of the most important of the cities of the Southwest. I had arrived there late in the evening. People were coming into the city by train-loads to attend the races. On my arrival, instead of going to one of the hotels, I went directly to the Young Men's Christian Association. I had learned, by that time, of the great value of the Associations as sources of information and help to strangers. There is no more practical benefit which the Associations throughout the country are conferring than simply making it known that they are ready to give welcome and counsel to any man who finds himself in their neighborhood without friends to turn to. Though the Secretary in this instance was very busy, he left his directors' meeting to give me advice as to lodging for the night, telephoned to one hotel after another, and then finally, when answers from each place came, " Every room full, on account of the races," offered me, half humorously, half seriously, a place on one of the reading-room tables for the night. Thanks to him, I did finally find a supper and a real bed. In the meantime, while I was hesitating to go out into the storm, he talked to me very frankly about certain phases of the religious life of the city.

" The churches here are after the individual. There is a recognized need for more social work. The ministers here recognize this weakness; but they feel more especially the lack of spirituality in the churches themselves." To illustrate this lack of spirituality he spoke of the way in which all church work suffered during the racing season. To his personal knowledge, " women who are church members go to the races and instruct their children how to bet. One deacon," he said, "was called in for help on Association work, and sent word that he had a sick headache — result of losing thirty dollars (a small sum, but the deacon, though rich, was ' close ') at the races. Yes, —— is a tough place — not because of open vice, but because of low standards among church people."

Certainly the city and indeed the whole region for scores of miles around seemed to be horse-mad; and I could well believe that what the Secretary told me, after making all allowance for possible personal bias in moral judgment, was not unfair. Those churches in the South and Southwest which especially pride themselves on the fact that they are stalwart in doctrine are not, so far as I could see, strong in moral fiber or rich in spiritual life. There are three elements that ought to be well balanced in all religious life: a measurable degree of intellectual certainty, moral conduct based on fundamental principles, and that sense of personal relationship to God which is usually termed spiritual experience. In the Southwest intellectual certainty was very manifest; moral conduct was emphasized, but seemed to be determined by more or less dogmatic precepts generally acquiesced in rather than by unifying principle; and spiritual experience was confined to a vague assurance that the future condition of one who maintained his intellectual certainty and followed the accepted moral precepts would not be endangered. In other words, the religion of the Southwest seemed to be the religion of the South largely stripped of its charm.

At the beginning of my trip some one told me that there was no better reflector of the religious life of the Southern people than the provincial religious papers. My experience confirmed this. The reason for this fact is not far to seek. The Southern people are not great readers. Even the clergymen of St. Louis, so I was told at a denominational book-store, buy but few books. The dwellers in the small towns and the country regions of the South, whose access to literature is more difficult and whose means for purchase are small, are the more dependent for their reading upon their denominational papers.

I came across one of these clearing-houses of religious thought in one of the important cities of the Southwest. It was the office of a Baptist weekly paper. When I entered, the editor, an elderly man with a long gray beard, looked up at me over his spectacles. I stated my errand and the name of the paper I represented. At the mention of The Outlook his face grew grave and somewhat severe. Very courteously, however, he gave me one or two copies of his paper and presented me with some statistics concerning his denomination in the State; but as for vouchsafing any expression of his ideas or point of view — not a word. He was as reticent as a diplomat. Soon a young man entered. The editor introduced him as his son, and put me into his hands. The son was no more communicative than his father, though equally courteous. At last, as if he could no longer withhold, he roundly said:

" We used to read The Outlook with great pleasure, when it was liberal: but now it has flopped on public questions."

This frankness broke the ice. For the rest of the morning there was no diplomacy. The trouble he took in giving up his work to talk with me and in taking me from one place to another to introduce me to representative men was one of the many demonstrations I have had that people are responsive to any one who they believe is trying to see from their point of view. Before I left the office both the editor and his son expressed a very genuine and cordial interest in the purpose of The Outlook to give, not an array of religious statistics, but a series of pictures of religious life in America.

In the conversation of these men there was no

suggestion of interest in what is called spiritual life. There was not even any use of cant terms, which may be called the blank cartridges of the Church militant; no hint that religion had to do with character, except as it involved stalwart adherence to a faith that had once for all been delivered to the saints. Nor was there any recognition of the effect which religion might have on the social life of men. Indeed, when I made an inquiry on this point, I was told that there were no social problems there! Happy city of over thirty thousand, without a social problem to disturb its Christian people! This was the reason given for the fact that the churches devoted all their attention to the con-version of the individual. This "conversion" was attained when the individual intellectually accepted certain dogmas and publicly identified himself with some church. Under these two divisions, doctrine and organization, could be included all that I found characteristic of the religious life of the Southwest, as expressed not only by what these two editors said, but, with perhaps one or two exceptions, by what I heard on every hand. The political ideas of my inter-locutor consistently reinforced his religious con-ceptions. He was, of course, a Democrat, and

was an active member of his party organization.
He measured political life, first, by political
doctrines—the formulas of faith that had once
for all been delivered to the fathers of the Republic—and, second, by his party, which apparently could do no wrong. His religious creed
was like his political platform—not subject to
interrogation. Any one who questioned either
was "more liberal," or, as he preferred to say,
"looser"—both terms of opprobrium. His
Church was, like his party, the embodiment of
righteousness and safety. Those who belonged
to other parties and other churches were mistaken—that was all that need be said about
them. As for those who belonged to no party
and no church—well, we did not discuss such
people. To hold an intellectual position involving self-contradiction seemed to cause him no
mental disturbance. At best, if there was to
be any reconciliation between theory and fact,
it was the facts that had to be brought into
conformity with the theories, not the theories
to the facts. He was urgent that the Filipinos
be given at once full political rights; and when
I asked him to harmonize that opinion with the
suppression by his party of the rights of the
negroes, he replied, "Oh, the negro has his po-

litical rights here." It happened that that day was election day; and the paper reported nearly six times as many Democratic as Republican votes. I wanted to find out what had become of the negro vote. So the next day I inquired of a negro, who had the confidence of the white people because he was emphatically not a politician, whether he ever voted. "Not now," he answered. "Would you be allowed to vote?" "Yes," he said with hesitation; "but," he added discreetly, "you know I don't want to go into politics." "Do the negroes here generally vote?" I persisted. "Yes." "Are their votes counted?" "Yes." "Out?" "Yes"; and he shrugged his shoulders, smiled, and changed the subject.

Now, the young Baptist editor had no intention of misrepresenting facts to me; but his political doctrine needed certain facts for its support, and therefore, he inferred, such the facts must be. In religious matters his mental attitude was the same. His theory of what his denomination ought to do was firmly established. Inasmuch as that theory was that the denomination should concern itself only for bringing about individual conversions, there could be no social problems. To make up for his lack of interest in the actual facts of life which affect religion (regarded as a spirit of life or a Christ-like spirit in the life of to-day), he evinced a very great deal of interest in the maintenance of the most minute details of doctrine. Baptism, of course, was, according to his belief, essential to Christian discipleship[1]; and also, of course, it was not baptism unless it was immersion. But even thus stated the doctrine was too general. "Southern Baptists, you know," he said, " are strongly opposed to alien immersion — that is, we deny the validity of the rite as performed by 'Disciples.' There is no laxity on this point. Northern Baptists are looser in this respect; but, partly because they are good-

---

[1] This phrase " Christian discipleship," though expressing precisely what I mean, is evidently open to misunderstanding, as a number of letters I have received since the first publication of this chapter have indicated. I therefore take this opportunity of saying — what seems too obvious to be incorporated into the text — that " Christian discipleship " is not here used as a synonym of "conversion " or "regeneration," but includes open *and adequate* acceptance *and confession* of the lordship and authority of Christ. Every rigorous Baptist insists that baptism is an indispensable part of even elementary obedience to Christ, and that church membership, of which baptism is a prerequisite, is an indispensable part of open confession of Christ. It is not surprising, however, that Baptists have protested against the idea which they have read into my statement, for that is the very point on which they take issue with the " Disciples." The latter — at least those of the extreme type — declare that baptism is a prerequisite to " regeneration," while the former owe their origin and existence as a sect largely to their protest against all forms of the doctrine of "baptismal regeneration " on the ground that it is a superstition. The letters I have received on this subject afford illustration of the intensity of doctrinal controversy between the sects in the region I have designated as the Edge of the Southwest.

humored, those who come here fall into our ways, and, by correspondence with friends at home in the North, produce a reflex influence there for greater doctrinal soundness. The insistence on doctrine is continued here unabated."

This hint at the controversial origin of this dogmatic spirit of the Southwest was characteristic. It was illustrated by a conversation I had with a cultivated lady who had been born and bred in Kentucky, but had lived in another State to the south and west for many years. She told me that her father and mother were Disciples, or " Christians " (as the followers of Alexander Campbell are variously called). As is generally known, " Campbellities " (the name which, though repudiated by themselves, is the only one that is distinctive) declare that they are not a denomination; that they have no creed but the New Testament and no doctrines but the commands of Jesus. They are, however, as insistent upon immersion as are the Baptists, and have very decided opinions about the relation between repentance and faith. Under the influences of this form of belief this lady was educated. Her parents gave her a New Testament and told her to read it and determine for herself what her belief should be. In that region the Baptists were the other aggressive sect. Just because these two denominations were so nearly alike in general matters of belief, their differences in details of doctrines made them and still make them the more intense in theological conflict. She exercised her right of private judgment, not by formulating her own faith, but by deciding between the tenets of opposing sects. And she chose the dogmas of the Baptists. Her belief was, therefore, the outcome of theological conflict, and, like a conqueror who has won new territory only after battle and privation, she guarded her hard-won spoils with severe and jealous vigilance. In her belief, Christianity was a Law to be obeyed — not a new motive to form character and determine conduct, but an external command which required unquestioning submission. Her chief interest in talking with me was, as she phrased it, "to find out what a thoughtful Pedobaptist would say in defense of his belief." When I began to tell what I thought such "a Pedobaptist would say," I found her ready with her proof-texts and her answers; until I soon felt myself, too, growing eager for the encounter. For that moment I understood and entered into the spirit of the religion of the Southwest. How tragic the outcome of such a spirit may be, those who have read James Lane Allen's "Reign of Law" can understand. Sometimes the outcome is not only tragic but almost grotesque, as was the case of a man whom I met in the extreme South. He had been bred in this Edge of the Southwest, and had been imbued with its spirit; but, finding nothing beautiful in it, rejected it *in toto*, and in doing so rejected Christianity itself. But so strong was the influence of his early training that he continued to find his most delightful avocation to consist in writing controversial essays on New Testament exegesis, and to-day has some considerable reputation as a theologian.

As a consequence of this atmosphere of controversy, an evangelist who disregards distinctions of dogma and makes his appeal both intellectually simple and frankly emotional is apt to be very effective in the Southwest. This was illustrated by an experience of mine in Little Rock, Arkansas. I had dropped in one evening at a prayer-meeting in a Baptist church. There were very few present; apparently I was the only stranger. An elderly gentleman with a patriarchal beard and a very benignant face took charge of the meeting in the absence of the pastor. After reading a psalm he turned toward me and asked me to offer prayer. With this unexpected request I of course willingly complied. Two or three took part in the meeting, one of whom was a very young man of somewhat self-important bearing, who uttered a most rhetorical jeremiad against the Christians of the city because they did not go to prayer-meeting, and closed with a threat that God in his wrath would burn them all up. At the close of the meeting the elderly gentleman who had been the leader at once came to me, welcomed me, inquired who I was, and, after hearing of my purpose, greatly to my astonishment offered me the hospitality which he and his gracious wife later extended to me in their sumptuous home. He was a former Governor of the State and a prominent officer of his church — indeed, had been ordained as a Baptist preacher.

"May I ask how you had the confidence to call on a stranger for prayer?" I asked.

"Oh," he replied, "any one who comes into a little prayer-meeting like this may be presumed to be able to lead in prayer." (That and the incident of the drummer with the Bible chart tell a great deal about religious conditions in the Southwest.) "But," the Governor protested, "you must not judge us by this little meeting. There's a revival going on in the Methodist church, and most of our people are over there. I should advise you to go."

When I reached the church, I found it crowded. People were standing in the aisles. On the platform a big man, with a voice that had the volume of a diapason and the *timbre* of a hautboy, was exhorting the audience. He had the instincts of a dramatic orator, and he showed them as he told a very simple story. Grown men throughout the audience were wiping their eyes with their handkerchiefs. The charming young girl in the story had divested herself of her finery and had made the old folks comfortable, had touched their hearts by her affection, and then had bidden farewell, when the evangelist turned, and, with his face and arms uplifted, declared how much richer, fuller, more self-denying was the love of Christ, and then, reaching out toward the congregation, seemed to single out here and there an individual to whom he appealed to accept this love and become Christ's. Then, after a hymn,

came the " after-meeting," when he called upon
his hearers to confess their faith.   With homely
illustration, and without a reference to theological formulas, he insisted upon the simplicity of
Christianity.   While the choir and congregation sang softly, he continued his appeals, and,
as one by one many people came forward —
men, women, and children — he took them by
the hands and asked for them the prayers of
believers.   That many of his methods were
meretricious and most of his ethical appeals
were fanatical did not weigh for an instant
against the simplicity of his gospel and its emphasis upon the personal — yes, and, if you will
have it so, the emotional — relationship between
the human life and God.   It was to hear this
that people had fled in throngs from the discord
of sects.   But back to the atmosphere of controversy they had to go — it may be imagined
with what confusion of mind.

Between the North and East on the one hand
and the Southwest on the other, the city of St.
Louis is a great commercial, industrial, moral,
and religious vortex.   The produce of the great
central plains of the continent gathers there for
distribution to Southern markets.   Factories
send their wares out to a varied population.

The ethical ideals of South and North, West and East, there find spontaneous expression. The religious conceptions of foreign-born Roman Catholics, of Western pioneers, of Southern conservatives, and of New England Puritans mingle and sometimes blend. It was, therefore, almost inevitable that there I should find expressed in its most extreme form the reaction from the individualism dominant and relentless in the Southwest. The group of men with whom I lunched one day — an editor, a manufacturer, a clergyman, a librarian, and a mechanic (one a product of the slums, another of the hemp-fields, another from the East, another from Scandinavia) — each unlike the others in nativity, training, occupation, and creed — all agreed that religion was something very different from that which the churches represented; that it was wholesome and normal only as it impelled men to live more wholesomely and normally with their fellow-men. As one of them — it was the editor, I think — put it, "The Bible begins in a garden and ends in a city. Not Eden, but the New Jerusalem, is the ideal." The "social gospel" was the only gospel they believed in — the "two or three *gathered together.*"

One of these men, whom I have called a mechanic, began life in Kentucky. By his parents he was brought up to be a stalwart "Disciple." On the corner of his father's farm was erected a meeting-house of the Disciples, to be a beacon in the midst of a region overwhelmed by the darkness of Baptist error. He told me that from the time he was eight years of age he carried about in his pocket a copy of the New Testament — not for devotional reasons, by any means, but for purposes of self-defense, so that whenever he met a Baptist he could whip it out and supply to his adversary proof-texts in support of the faith that was in him; and valiantly did he wield this sword of the Spirit. As he grew older he left the farm to prepare himself for the ministry of the Disciples; and at last became a preacher in full standing. After an experience in various pulpits, he was forced to the conclusion that the churches were not influencing the real workers of the world — or at least of his world; were not even acquainted with their lives. So, withdrawing from the ministry — not because he lacked sympathy with the Church, but in order to be sure that he would be no burden to his denomination — he turned to manual labor as a means of supporting his family. He went into Arkansas, with a library consisting of Shakespeare, Dante, Homer, and the Bible, and "farmed it." Of his life there he had many amusing stories to tell. From one occupation to another he went in his search for knowledge of humanity. When I met him, he was an apprentice in a machine-shop. In the evening he superintended a Jewish social settlement. He was president of a society for excavating mammoth remains. He told me that one of his sons, a boy of sixteen or thereabouts, wanted to keep a peanut-stand; he gave his consent, and the boy set up his stand in one of the roughest places of the city. He feared no harm for his son, because he had faith in the boy's home training, and he believed his acquisition of real knowledge of the city life would do him good. All this time this man has kept his membership in the little "Disciple" church on his father's farm in Kentucky, has contributed to its support, and at least once a year goes there to preach. Never have I met a man who has adjusted himself and has kept himself adjusted to so many grades of society, who has had a larger range of interests, and who has had a simpler, surer faith. As we strolled from one place to another in the city — now in a little restaurant where he knew the proprietor and his family, now in the " Reform Rooms," where we argued with some acquaintances of his about Socialism and Single Tax, now in one or two quiet saloons which he showed me as typical " workingmen's clubs," now in the basement lodging-house of the Salvation Army, to which we took a poor deaf and dumb young fellow — he kept throughout his imperturbable spirit, his unchangeable sanity of mind and Christian feeling.

It was in St. Louis, also, that I met a man who had come to this same point by a road from an exactly opposite direction. He had been a newsboy on the East Side of New York, and afterwards a mechanic in a factory. He, too, saw that the workers of *his* world were not known by the churches. So, as one who at least knew the point of view of workingmen, he decided to become a minister, that he might bring the life of Christ into the life of artisans and mechanics. Simple in heart and very modest, he would tell me little about himself; but on Easter evening, when I attended the service at his mission, joined the crowded congregation of the poor, heard his very human account of the death and resurrection of Jesus, listened to the music rendered under the direction of his gifted wife — music that was far better in real musical value than the more ornate choral service I had heard in a wealthy uptown church that very morning — and met some of his congregation after the service, I learned more from him than he could tell, or perhaps could know.

These two men represent the hope of the Southwest for a real and a growing religious life.

KANSAS

VIII

KANSAS

THE wide main street of the little city was
lined with farm horses and wagons, coated
up to flank and hub with mud. It was Saturday, and the sidewalks were crowded with farmers. The men and boys were such as may be
seen any day waiting for the mail on many a
village corner in Maine. They showed the
same signs of clean, honest labor in the sun
and on the soil; they had the same set mouths
that can very well say "I will" or "I won't,"
but can convey that idea just as well without
speaking; the same lines about the eyes that
betoken equal shrewdness in swapping either
stories or horses; the same bearing that suits
equally a hoe and a rifle, and that for practical
purposes has borne comparison with the military
swagger of the Hessian and the Spaniard. One

can generally recognize the veritable Yankee, whether he is raising potatoes in Aroostook County, Maine, or making butter in a valley of the Catskills, or driving a reaper in a Western wheat-field. I saw scores of him that dismal Saturday afternoon in this Kansas town.

I had just come into Kansas from Missouri. There was nothing to remind me that I was in the same country except the mud; but even in this respect there was a difference—in Kansas the mud was deeper. In the presence of this one ubiquitous evidence of unimproved Nature it was possible to understand why Kansans feel justified in thinking so well of themselves. In their State it is only Nature that is vile. Even in the neighborhood of the railroads everything that bears the human mark — house or sidewalk, cultivated field or shop—speaks of cleanliness, order, and industry. Except for the street lights of natural gas (which it is cheaper to leave burning all day than to extinguish and relight) and the scarcity of trees, any one of the villages I passed through would be inconspicuous in New England. The nearness of Missouri has by its contrast contributed to a certain self-complacency characteristic of Kansas. It is the quality of piety in Kansas to thank God that you are not as other men are, beer-drinkers, shiftless, habitually lynchers, or even as these Missourians; you work six days in the week, and pay taxes rather than let saloons pay licenses.

Down the street among these transplanted Yankees, I made my way to the office of a lawyer of the city. Like other Kansans, I found him thinking of religious life in terms of concrete moral problems. He had not a word to say about doctrines. I have actually forgotten to what denomination he belonged. His strongest religious feelings found expression in his support of prohibition. He argued for it, not mainly on the ground of expediency, but on the ground of conscience. For this reason his opinions were not in the least affected by the fact, which he frankly admitted, that in some cities of the State the law was openly violated. Prohibition was essentially right, a part of the moral law, and had the sanction of all who supported religion. He disbelieved in the principle of local option because it put the burden of recurrent agitation upon the "temperance people"; in his opinion it was unfair to put this burden upon the people who were right, depriving them of just so much time from "legitimate business." Under prohibition, even unenforced, the burden of positive agitation was laid upon the liquor-dealers, who were manifestly wrong, and who therefore ought to bear the burden.

This illustrates the contrast between Kansas and the contiguous Southwest. The difference is not that between the dogmatic and the un-dogmatic. In the Southwest religious life is marked, as I have described in a previous arti-cle, by doctrinal dogmatism. In Kansas re-ligious life is marked by dogmatism also; only it is not doctrinal, but moral. There is another difference. In the Southwest religious dogma-tism is a choppy sea; for doctrines of one sect conflict with the doctrines of another. In Kansas religious dogmatism is a strong cur-rent, for church people of all names are prac-tically agreed as to what moral courses are unquestionably Christian. It is true that Kansas is not by any means wholly free from the dogmatism of creed. It is also true that one of the most relentlessly dogmatic asser-tions as to moral conduct which I have ever heard was made in Arkansas. But in the main the " Higher Criticism " is the representative heresy of the Southwest, while that of Kansas is Beer.

When I inquired what the churches were doing to supply a substitute for the saloon, I could find no positive information. As in doctrine so in morals, it is much easier to combat a heresy than to construct a faith. The lawyer of whom I have spoken had others to agree with him that in constructive moral effort the churches were weak. Kansas, however, is an essentially rural State, and therefore does not feel the need of public centers of social life. Most boys in Kansas, I was told, can grow to manhood without knowing what a saloon is. The general impression which I received from many people and various experiences as to the moral and religious life in the rural communities (which dominate the State) may be expressed in the words of a business man, a fellow-townsman of the lawyer:

"Some of the young people are leaving the country — even the best of them — but those that remain on the farms are doing well. Until two or three years ago there was a decline in prosperity; but now the young men have taken hold, and are paying off debts, and in an amazingly short time are making great profits. The churches are also growing; interest in religion is increasing. Often churches are crowded — a hundred where you might expect forty. I think that the hard financial times were responsible for a great deal that was thought to be dishonest. Now, however, moral life, in the widest sense, is improving. Whether all this moral and religious improvement is simply the result of prosperity or not it is hard to say, but I believe it is real."

It was a Presbyterian minister who first told me that I should find among the Methodists the most typical country churches, and introduced me to a Methodist minister, who very kindly arranged a short tour with a local preacher. The dismal drizzle of the afternoon turned into rain, and when nine o'clock came with no sign of the local preacher I was about to conclude that weather did not permit. Just then, in the darkness, the local preacher drove to the door. He was a student from a Methodist college, who spent his Sundays and vacations in ministering to the scattered population of neighboring districts.

"I am afraid it will be impossible for me to take you along," he said. And, sure enough, the mud on the wheels of his buggy banished all thought of making his pony draw us both. Finally, after agreeing to provide a pair of horses for the trip, and to speak to his people in his place on the morrow (for his reluctance to preach in the presence of a stranger proved to be as much of an obstacle to the plan as the mud was), I prevailed upon him to take me with him. When I expressed my hesitation at intruding myself on the hospitality of his people, he laughed me out of my fears. Any one of the homes in his district, he told me, was always ready to receive him at any time, and anybody he might happen to have with him. That was the way he lived on Sundays and during vacations. He had no parsonage or regular boarding-place. He had his traveling-bag, his horse, and his buggy. As he drove around the region, any house near which he happened to be at meal-time or night he would make his home for the time being. This time, he said, we should stay at the County Infirmary (what in New England is called the Poor Farm), the superintendent of which was a parishioner of his. So off we drove our hired horses through the dark, with no sign of road on the flat country to guide us; except as we felt the jar of turning out of the deep ruts, there was nothing to indicate that we were not driving over a pathless prairie.

At last the gleam of light from the Infirmary reached us through the darkness. At the door we were warmly bidden welcome. The Superintendent was a tall, well-knit man, clean shaven; his face would have satisfied Rembrandt. He had been a veritable pioneer. Starting from the East in his boyhood, he went westward by degrees, always keeping just ahead of the railroad until it overtook him in Kansas; there he settled for life. It was the incidental in his narrative, which he told with a certain quiet dignity that was very convincing, that expressed, more forcibly than any explicit statement could express, his stalwart faith. And as he told little tales and anecdotes about the inmates of the poorhouse and about the unfortunates who applied there from time to time for food and shelter, his religious feeling showed the sort of tenderness and human sympathy that is possible only in the most virile natures. His view of the present religious conditions in his State was most hopeful; his confidence in the character of the younger generation was buoyant. In this respect he was representative of almost all whom I met in Kansas. The New England

country Yankee is apt to be a religious hypo-
chondriac; he spiritually "enjoys poor health";
he is reminiscent of the good old times, and
finds a doleful pleasure in predicting general
religious catastrophe. The Kansas Yankee —
such is the force of environment — is his direct
opposite. When, for instance, my host the
Superintendent told of the days of the anti-
slavery struggle, his eyes brightened and he
drew himself together as if ready for a renewal
of it; but when he spoke of the young people of his acquaintance and their efforts and
achievements, he showed in his quiet way even
greater assurance and enthusiasm.

Sunday broke clear and sunny. We had
three miles or so to drive to Wesley Chapel.
Never have I seen such mud. The ruts were
no deeper simply because the hubs refused to
let the wheels sink lower. When we were yet
a mile from the chapel there was a snap, and
the horses stopped with a jerk. The whiffle-
tree had broken. In a few minutes my companion, the local preacher, had the fracture
bound with a strap from my camera-case.
When we resumed our journey, I inquired
whether, with the road in such condition, it was
worth while to go on. Would there be any-

body there? I was assured there would be a very fair-sized congregation. But there was no village or settlement near by? No; the people lived in isolated farm-houses. When the chapel came into view, I could see horses and wagons standing near it; and when we approached it, I discovered that they lined the road on either side for several rods. Among them were several saddled horses. The congregation within the little chapel was by no means a small one. There was a surprisingly large proportion of young people. There was also a conspicuously large proportion of men. In decorum and in intelligent attention the congregation was remarkably superior to the ordinary country congregation of New England. Upon inquiry after service I learned that, with the exception of the members of one household who had walked from their home half a mile distant, all in this congregation had driven or ridden — many of them for three miles or more — over those wretched roads. I never heard of a present-day New England community which could match that. Yet I was convinced by many kinds of testimony that this was by no means a remarkable Kansas community.

We were entertained, together with two

other guests— one of them the son of a "Professor of Typewriting"—in the neighboring tiny and rather primitive farm-house. The rotary cream separator in the dining-room betokened the progressive farmer. Sunday was evidently no bugbear to the three small boys of the family. The Sunday atmosphere of this home that day was surcharged with a very wholesome, happy spirit. Perhaps the result can best be described by saying that it was a combination of Puritanism and the prairie.

The trait of expectancy, if it may be so called, which is characteristic of the religious feeling I noticed in the distinctively rural portions of the State, was equally marked in its colleges. Kansas is dotted with colleges, mainly, of course, denominational. In them the churches exert an influence very much concentrated, and at scarcely one remove. Under these circumstances it is not to be expected that education would result as yet in skepticism, and until the skeptical spirit appears there is nothing in Kansas to attack the spirit of religious hopefulness. The State University is an exception in that it has a reputation for irreligion. So far as I could ascertain, this reputation has been fostered mainly by the denominational colleges, most of which find the State University a formidable competitor, and is undeserved. Justification, however, for that reputation was many times offered to me on the ground that in the University at Lawrence there was no compulsory chapel, and that the churches were not moved by self-interest, as in the case of denominational colleges, to make the religious training of the students their business. My visit to the University of Kansas, brief though it was, enabled me to see that these two facts were quite as favorable as detrimental to religion. The optional system of chapel attendance, so both officers and students testified, had operated to create sincerity and spontaneity in religious life. I admit that I possibly gave credence to this testimony the more readily because it accorded with my previous conviction; but that, of course, does not alter in the least the fact of the testimony. As to the influence of the churches upon the life of the students, it was evident that the relation between the University and the churches, as described to me, was closer there than I had found to exist in any college town I had then visited on this trip. The fact, as reported to me, that during the summer, when the students had left for the vacation, a number of the churches were seriously weakened, was creditable alike to the churches and to the University.

Illustrative of the spontaneity of the students' religious life was the character of the University Young Men's Christian Association. A benefactor of the University had given the Association two small brick houses. With these in its possession the Association wisely saw its opportunity to supply a need that the lack of dormitories occasioned; so it decided to make of its "plant," not the ordinary Association rooms, but club-houses similar to those maintained by college fraternities. In order, however, to avoid the formation of a religious-social clique, the managers, with evident tact, chose as residents representative students of the University. As the rooms were in every way desirable, the beneficial effect of this broad-minded policy was immediately felt. As a consequence, the Young Men's Christian Association became a leading factor in the development of the entire college life; and religion, far from being accepted as a separate segment in the life of the University, has become identified with wholesomeness in athletics and other recreation and with soundness of scholarship. The Young Women's

Christian Association has likewise achieved leadership in the life of the women of the University. The officers of this Association whom I met united with their ingenuous religious earnestness rare personal charm, while the representatives of the Young Men's Christian Association were thoroughly vigorous fellows, who bore none of the familiar pietistic scars on their Christian faith.

The man who, of all whom I met in Kansas, seemed to have the best-formulated understanding of the State was a professor in a Congregational college. A native of the East, a graduate of Yale, he looked at facts in their perspective. After my talk with him I was more than ever impressed with the truth that the present religious and moral character of Kansas was only the persistence of the temper that was wrought into the people during the days of Eli Thayer's Emigrant Company, the Wakarusa War, and the Lecompton Constitution. The settlers of the State had for their purpose primarily to make, not a fertile soil fruitful, but an unsettled soil free. They were not content with talking about anti-slavery; they were first of all intent on doing something to resist slavery's encroachments. To-day the same spirit exists. Even the most talkative Kansas idealist — and the talkative one in my experience was an exception — can always be found to have his idealism firmly fastened to a peg driven deep in the earth. The Beecher Bible and Rifle Company still in the spirit hovers over Kansas like the horses and chariots of fire round about Elisha.

An opportunity I valued highly was afforded me in a conversation with a man who through his position had intimate acquaintance with the intellectual, moral, and religious life of the State. He was full of racy and brisk expressions.

"You cannot understand Kansas without seeing a railroad map of the State. The Santa Fé system is spread out like fingers; it has the State under its hand. That is Kansas to-day. But when I was eight years old, Topeka was nothing but straggling, scrawny topography. The Santa Fé may not be a moral force, but it explains the State. Scarcely more than a generation ago the only inhabitants here were wolves, prairie-dogs, and grasshoppers. Why, every tree that you see anywhere here is an artificial product." I thought of the shady lawn-bordered streets of Lawrence. "Every brick and pavement that goes down, every board that you see, has come from outside the State. We haven't centuries behind us. We are a thing of yesterday, and not very early in the morning, either. We haven't had time to do anything but build our 'plant.' Men haven't had time to formulate their ideas; even in towns they think more about plows than anything else. And we are still in the process. Almost any day you will see a little house on wheels being moved out to the edge of the city. It has been sold to a negro; the man who built it is busy putting up a better one in its place. But when the time for settling intellectual problems comes, they will be settled wholesomely, not tackled in the mulish fashion as in Missouri. There's too much beer in Missouri; they work there too much in the breeching. That's another handicap. We're behind Missouri, a big, hulking barrier between here and the East, and everything comes through or around. On the other side Kansas has turned mother for the free lands of Oklahoma. The western part of Kansas, besides, is like another State — mostly uninhabited. Crops there are uncertain. Curious weeds grow there that drop round seed-balls that are rolled along by the wind. You see a line of these rolling weeds moving steadily over the ground, like a line of cavalry, until they come bump against a wire fence. They look like kobolds and trolls of the under-world; they start you into uncontrollable laughter like that of Homer's gods. It is the eastern part of the State that is the real Kansas." Mr. Sheldon, who gained wide repute a few years ago as setting forth the question, "What would Jesus do?" as the supreme interest of the Christian, he cited as typical of the State. "As soon as Mr. Sheldon gets the tugs on he wants to get them hitched to a cart filled with 'niggers' from Tennesseetown. He wants to switch men off from speculative questions to the practical— from ' are there few to be saved?' to 'strive to enter in at the strait gate.' It's a mean man that would suspect his motives."

This I found corroborated in the brief interview I had with Mr. Sheldon. Personally he was extremely modest, but in his moral convictions absolutely confident as to just what Jesus would drink, just how Jesus would conduct a newspaper or manage a church. Indeed, he has the courage of his convictions, and has been willing to undertake to show to others by his own actions just what particular things the Christian life involves. In Kansas this is saved from being pharisaism by the fact that Kansas people think in the concrete and accept this method as the normal way of expressing truth.

There is nothing abstract about Kansas. Even ideality there becomes concrete. There are signs of an approaching time when Christianity there will be identified with motive and spirit rather than with precept. In the meantime those ministers and laymen who are magnifying specific reforms as the substance of Christianity are serving a highly useful purpose, for they are using concrete terms, which everybody who hears them understands, and making them religious.

THE EASTERN WEST

IX

THE EASTERN WEST

"WHAT is your impression of our State?" was the question asked of me in almost every State I visited. To that question I formulated no answer until I came to Iowa. There, after I was assured that my frank opinion was desired, I was ready to answer in one word — "Monotony."

"Yes," came the reply; "we Iowans believe in the virtue of *uniformity*."

Although I accepted the rebuke as to choice of words, I secretly continued to think Iowa somewhat monotonous as well as merely uniform. Granting, however, the modification in language which the rebuke suggests, I believe that that answer can be applied, in somewhat less degree, to the religious life of all that part of the country called the Middle West. True religion and undefiled, in the eyes of the dwellers in that part of the West, is to conform to certain standards of thought and conduct. Such religion is displayed in the services of the churches. Among Episcopalian churches, on the one hand, ritualism flourishes; in non-ritualistic churches, on the other hand, there thrives an equally strong conventionality, though of opposite appearance. The surplice is inadequately replaced by the white tie; the vaulted nave by the semicircular auditorium with opera-chairs; images of the saints by blackboards, maps, and stereopticon screens; Gregorian tones by an easily recognizable type of anthems furnished by publishing houses at so much a month. These and other like symbols of religion which I might name are not all found in every church, but they might be combined to form an ideal to which most of the churches which I saw are tending. In religious thinking, too, conformity is the rule. The questioning spirit which will not down even in the Southwest exists also in this land of broad acres and growing cities, but it is on the defensive. When it becomes too active, it crystallizes into one of numerous new and strange sects, of which the land yields more than its share, and ceases to have any portion in religion pure and undefiled. Eloquence, of a sort that must meet the test of the summer assembly platforms which are within reach of most of the people, rather than thought, is the primary essential in making a sermon acceptable. The successful minister must have business enterprise. The preacher who " warms up to his subject" and is efficient in raising a debt "challenges admiration."

The most illuminating comments made to me on these conditions were those of a young clergyman who understood them better than either most visitors to the Middle West, who have perspective but no sympathy, or most dwellers in the Middle West, who have sympathy but no perspective. This clergyman understood these conditions sympathetically, because his early life had been spent among them; but he had gained perspective by his course of study in the East and in Germany, and his successful ministry in the pioneer regions of the Northwest.

" In my little church," he said to me, " I have the attention and support of the thinking people; but that is not enough. When you divide a small church like this, you've weakened your working force. One of my deacons told me that the trouble with my sermons was that I didn't get 'hot under the collar'!" The fact that this deacon, a representative man in the community, could not see the grotesqueness of his suggestion that a man of such absolute sincerity and real earnestness as his minister should work himself up into a pseudo-oratorical display, was of itself enough to explain why thoughtful earnestness and open-minded sincerity are not (to use an appropriate commercial phrase) a very valuable ministerial asset nowadays in the Middle West.

The combination of formalism and enterprise, of conventionality and "hustle," is what gives distinctive character to this large region which may be called the Eastern West. It has come into its enterprise by inheritance, for not long ago it was pioneer country. But with the years its unconventional manners have become stereotyped and developed into new conventions. The nonconformist has made of his nonconformity a new conformity. It is the history over again of the Protestant freeing himself from an infallible Church only to set up in its place an infallible Bible — of the Puritan fleeing from an established Church in England only to set up an establishment of his own in America.

So far as this conventionalizing process advanced that it already bears some of the marks which a similar process in the East bears. In several small towns of Illinois and Iowa I heard stories of the decrease of young people, of moral and religious indifference and even degeneration, and of what may be called anæmic civilization, which bore very close likeness to what I had observed in small towns and villages of New England. The star of empire, as it makes its way to the westward, seems to be a comet, and its tail is convention.[1]

An extreme case of this combination of conventionality and " hustle " was a service I attended in a United Presbyterian church. As is well known, the people of this denomination are extremely conservative in their theology. The one distinctive tenet, however, for which

[1] In a letter concerning this statement, a minister of the Middle West declares that he knows of no section in which the churches are " more free from convention than in this very region," and adds, in support of his statement, that the churches there are " ready for new ideas and new methods." In other words, this minister expresses the not uncommon idea — especially prevalent in the Middle West — that enterprise is equivalent to unconventionality. This, of course, is to confound conventionalism with traditionalism. Traditionalism is conformity to a usage or an idea because it is sanctioned by age; conventionalism is conformity to a usage or an idea because it is sanctioned by general concurrence. One of the ways in which conventionalism shows itself is in extreme readiness to adopt novelties. An ultra-fashionable woman adopts a new fashion without regard to its intrinsic beauty because she is conventional ; she adopts it when it first makes its appearance because she is also enterprising. Similarly some of the most enterprising churches are also the most conventional.

they are most generally known is their belief
that no hymns should be used in divine worship—none but the Psalms of the Old Testament. The argument is something like this:
The Psalter is incomparably the best hymn-book
ever written; the exclusive use of it bars out
trivial and sectarian hymns; and, more than
all, God has commanded its use, or, in the
words of one of the denomination's accredited
defenders, " Doesn't it look like God had given
us a hymn-book to sing from as well as a Bible
to preach from, and that we have no more right
to supplant the one than the other with a book
of our own composing? " Therefore only the
inspired language of the Psalms should be used
in singing praise to God. In this church which
I attended the hymn-book was made up of metrical versions of the Psalms set to tunes generally familiar in most American churches. The
service, except for the hymns, was in no way
remarkable. The pastor of the church was a
young man, eminent in his denomination, so I
was told, for one of his years. His sermon
was on the deity of Christ, and consisted of a
series of coördinate propositions, each purporting to prove his main point and each supported
by Scripture texts, which he quoted and cited

by chapter and verse as a lawyer cites cases in
addressing the judge. His citations averaged
about one a minute. Now for the evidence of
business enterprise. When the notices had
been given out, the pastor placed a blackboard
beside the pulpit and announced that he wanted
one hundred dollars raised that morning. He
then wrote " $100 " on the blackboard and
waited for contributions. A man in the congregation rose and stated that he would give
ten dollars. The minister thereupon announced
the man's name, drew a line through the "$100,"
and wrote underneath " $90." The first pledge
proved to be the largest. With each pledge
thereafter the minister placed a new figure on
the board, indicating at each step the amount yet
needed. When the last dollar was crossed off,
the minister continued the service, and at the
end of his sermon called on the man who had
subscribed ten dollars to lead in prayer. In the
Sunday-school as in the church service, metrical
versions of the inspired Psalms were exclusively
sung, but the music set to them was as unin-
spired as those which any hack writer of Sunday-school jingles ever perpetrated. There
being no infallible standard of divine music,
there seemed to be no need of following any

standard whatever. The brisk competition of other Sunday-schools evidently had to be met.

Less traditional and more enterprising was another church in the same city — the "Central Church of Christ," colloquially called " Camp-bellite," much to the displeasure of its members. This denomination, variously known also as " Christians " and " Disciples," [1] is one of the most aggressive of all religious bodies in the United States. In the city to which I have just referred, the Congregationalists had "the start," but their numbers, so I was told, had actually decreased; the Disciples, on the other hand, had established ten churches in eleven

---

[1] It is not my purpose in this book to go into denominational distinctions; but in the case of this denomination it is almost imperative to do so. The name " Campbellite " is distasteful to those to whom it is applied, because they claim to be followers, not of a man, but of the New Testament. They therefore want no distinctive name, desiring to be known only as Christians, Disciples of Christ, and as constituting Churches of Christ. The fact, however, that others, who repudiate this movement started by Alexander Campbell and hold rather to the teaching of a man by the name of Stone, have the desire to be similarly known makes it necessary to use a distinctive name. Inasmuch as the feeling between the followers of Stone and the followers of Campbell is intense to the degree of bitterness (as may easily be discovered by reading the journals of either sect), the terms " Campbellite " on the one hand, and " Stonite " or " New Light " on the other, have naturally arisen, and form convenient denominational designations. It would be easier to use a more acceptable name if either party had a uniform use as to name. The fact is, however, that the denomination called " Campbellite " is, for instance, in Ohio called " Disciples," in Illinois " Christians," in Iowa " Church of Christ"! yet it is not three denominations, but one denomination. " Campbellite " is the only distinctive title that applies to the denomination everywhere. In this chapter I shall use the term " Disciples," though it is neither distinctive nor universal.

years, and they were then all flourishing. The
spirit of the Disciple ministers may be indicated
by an anecdote told me by one of them about
another. The clergyman was asked whether
he were pastor of the biggest Protestant church
in the country. He replied, " I don't know and
don't care; I wish simply to be a servant." A
few moments later he was asked what the membership of his church was. He replied instantly:
" Two thousand three hundred and fifty-one
this morning ! " The growth of the Disciples
cannot be explained altogether by this eagerness for numbers, for, though it is especially
characteristic of this denomination, it is very
evident in other denominations — not least
among Congregationalists. Neither can this
growth be attributed to the denomination's
polity, for each local church of the Disciples,
like each local church of the Congregationalists, is supreme law unto itself. It can only be
attributed to the spirit of the Disciples, which
may be termed parochial unselfishness. Among
Congregationalists the local church is preëmi-
nently living unto itself. It may, and usually
does, give largely to missions, but its chief
interest is in its own prosperity. A small
Congregational church almost invariably feels

the competition, rather than the assistance, of a neighboring rich church of its own denomination. Its organist, if markedly efficient, is likely to receive from the richer church the offer of an increased salary; its social life is likely to suffer in comparison with the very distinct social life of its more elegant neighbor; its activities are likely to conflict with the activities of the church with larger resources. The parish of the larger Congregational church is seldom determined by geographical lines, but usually extends into the domains of other and smaller churches of its own denomination. This parochial selfishness of Congregational churches is not by any means confined to the Middle West; I could cite cases of it which I have observed in every part of the country I have visited where Congregational churches abound; but it is peculiarly noticeable where it stands in contrast with the parochial unselfishness of those which may be denoted by the rather inaccurate term Disciple churches. The Central Church of Christ is a marked example of this parochial unselfishness and its reward. Each of the other ten churches of the denomination has been organized by members of the Central Church, and by the assistance of that church has become a new center for the activity of Disciples. As the pastor of the church said to me, "I could have had three thousand members here, but I could not have done anything with them. This church is really stronger because it mothers other churches." While this Central Church has grown from 380 to 1600 in sixteen years, the total number of Disciples in the city has increased from 380 to 5300 in that time. As a consequence, this small army of Disciples presents a solid front, while the other denominations are periodically stirred up over their "proselyting."

At the time I was in the city, the periodical embroilment had just been created by the presence of a Disciple evangelist. Just "to show that there was no hard feeling" the ministers of the city invited this evangelist to address them at their weekly Monday meeting. Beginning his address with pleasant generalities about the unity of the Church, he skillfully led up to an argument in justification of the distinctive tenets as to church union held by his denomination. By this flank movement the parade-ground seemed suddenly transformed into a battlefield. Before the opposing forces had

time to rally, he made a new attack with the
weapon of prayer, beseeching the Lord that the
assembled ministers should not seek to save
their own souls, but only those of others. Thereupon, apparently in order to meet this last attack first, some one started the hymn,

> A charge to keep I have,
>   A God to glorify;
> A never-dying soul to save,
>   And fit it for the sky.

Then, as if to protest that this was, after all,
only a sham battle, some one else started

> Blest be the tie that binds
> Our hearts in Christian love.

After the hymns the meeting adjourned, the
Disciple theological students, who were there in
some numbers to support their champion, exult-
ing over the " vindication " of their undenomina-
tional denomination, the ministers generally discussing their helplessness when such tactics
were employed.

This Central Church of Christ, besides beget-
ting a large family of churches, has shown more
activity within its own parish than any other
church of the city.   I called on its pastor in his

office — rather than study — in the " Institute " connected, organically and locally, with the church. He was sitting at a roll-top desk, on which there rested a telephone. Several times while I was there he had to excuse himself to answer the bell and converse with some one who needed his advice or other assistance. Each time, as he hung up the receiver, he would turn to me and resume the conversation, where it had been interrupted, with businesslike clearness and incisiveness. Many little incidents revealed his almost detective-like capacity for getting at facts, understanding situations, and " sizing up" men. He afforded another of the many illus- trations of the truth that religious life, like all other life, is determined more by personality than by methods or doctrines or anything else. He showed himself at once a profound sympa- thizer with all who are feeling the pressure of hard social conditions, and a keen questioner as to the duty of the Church toward the relief of those conditions. That he had practical methods for getting acquainted with the views of organ- ized laboring men, and of employers and busi- ness men, he showed by the letters he had received, the questions he had circulated for information, and the topics he had preached on.

His church was evidently a busy one. A lay assistant was in charge every day all day long. The building contained two reading-rooms, each with its own function; a recreation-room, with games; class-rooms for the use of the Bible school, week-day classes, and various church clubs; and a gymnasium, besides the pastor's office, the church auditorium, and the lecture-room.

"The church may be called semi-institutional," said the pastor. "We find we have to give up some things. Language classes were advertised; enough pupils applied, but we found they were the kind that could go elsewhere. So we substituted other work; for instance, that for cash-boys. We got them by approaching the proprietors of the stores in which they worked. Result was very successful. In the suburban church the problem is how to use surplus energy; here all our energy can be used. Something is going on here all the time. We have a group of people who go to the —— Mission, another to the Old Women's Home, another to the Settlement. Our library has been made unnecessary by the establishment of the city library near by; so we have sent our Sunday-school books to the missions, and keep only religious literature for use in the study of the

Bible. Our gymnasium work, on the other hand, has not interfered with the Young Men's Christian Association, for we take boys it won't or can't take. Through the gymnasium we have had a number of boys come into the church. Is there a wide difference of theological opinion in the church? It is not discussed or emphasized; but there is absolute freedom, except as to the divinity of Christ. I know there is difference of belief about future punishment — probation, restoration, and brimstone. Baptism would seem to be an exception " — the Disciples are very strong advocates of immersion —" but that is really due to catholicity, for everybody agrees that immersion is baptism, but not everybody accepts sprinkling as valid. We advocate the form that is universally acknowledged." He expressed opinions that were in full accord with modern developments of theological thought, according to the discoveries of evolution and literary criticism of the Bible. " We have a course of Bible lectures," he added; " one of the speakers, a consummate Bible lecturer, stirred up the people to thinking." His emphasis, however, was all upon the practical work of relief of distress, effort for social betterment, and education.

This church is a type of the churches that are winning their way in the conventionalized portions of the West. Another church of the same type, but not by any means so obviously successful, I saw in a Wisconsin city. I had made an appointment to meet the pastor at the church, but missed my appointment because, when I reached the place to which I had been directed, I could see no sign of a church. After a fruitless search, I returned to the place and discovered that what I had taken to be an elegant club-house or apartment-house was in fact the church. Within, except for the main auditorium, the building was appropriate to its exterior—tasteful parlors, a good library, convenient class-rooms, two kitchens, office-rooms for the pastor and officers of the church, and a small theater, with stage complete. Its comparative inactivity was due to at least two causes; one was that, being a Congregational church, it did not have the coöperation of other churches; the other was that its success had in some respects threatened its ruin, for one after another of its projects had so outgrown the capacity of the church that separation became necessary, and energy formerly exercised under the church organization had necessarily been withdrawn.

The very appearance, therefore, of inactivity was in this instance a demonstration of the value that this church had in the community. Like the Disciple church I have described, but in far greater degree, this church was a leader away from conventional theological thought.

The direction from which constructive movements in religious thought and life in the Middle West are likely to come is indicated by certain signs of revolt against convention which form the subject of the next chapter.

THE REVOLT AGAINST
CONVENTION

X

THE REVOLT AGAINST CONVENTION

"OF all the men I've ever come across," remarked a commercial traveler who happened to be my seat-mate in a Western train, "ministers have the poorest sense of right and wrong. With one exception, in all the dealings I've had with ministers, I've come out at the little end."

The conversation was occasioned by the publication in a newspaper which one of us had of a report made by a number of clergymen who had gone to a military garrison to investigate the effects of the abolishment of the "canteen." The "investigation" had consisted largely in a violent wordy altercation between the commander of the garrison and the clergyman who was chairman of the committee, during which the chairman stated emphatically that he would never favor the resumption of the canteen even if its abolishment had proved detrimental to the troops. The report, which all the clergymen but one had signed, was, of course, adverse to the canteen. It was the willingness of these clergymen to be partisans in trying to uphold a conventional morality that had aroused my fellow-passenger's ire. Their partisanship was to him the more contemptible because it involved ignorance of facts which were not only familiar to him, but, in his opinion, easily ascertainable by any fair-minded man. When it transpired that the committee based its report in the main on the testimony of some saloon-keepers whose self-interest led them to agree with the clergymen in favoring the abolition of the canteen, my companion exclaimed, " That makes me hot under the collar! "

A railroad train is not a good place for gathering facts or statistics, but it is not a bad place for discovering specific illustrations of human nature. The very fact that neither of us expected to meet the other again left us both free to disregard those considerations of the future that are the chief cause of modifying or preventing the frank expression of opinion. In

this case, at any rate, I found in my fellow-
traveler a type of a great number of men, as I
had met them and talked with them, who find
in the conventional forms of religious life and
thought little with which to sympathize and
much with which to be irritated.   Not that
such men are uninterested in religion, nor
even in the Church and its ministers.   This
commercial traveler, for example, exasperated
as he was by this instance of ministerial nar-
rowness, volunteered expressions of high praise
for two ministers of his acquaintance. The fact
is, I found surprisingly little of that uncom-
promising prejudice against ministers and the
Church, which is often supposed to exist among
men of my traveling companion's stamp; on
the other hand, I found a generally prevalent
habit of judging ministers and the Church, not
by their conformity to conventional standards,
but by their fruits.

This does not mean that such men are greatly
impressed by numbers. The rapid growth of
Christian Science interests them, but does not
even begin to persuade them of its value.
Evidence, however, that Christian Science has
affected for good the character of some one
they know does more than interest them; it

arouses in them a respect for that cult and opens the door to persuasion. My seat-mate, for instance, remarked: " I have no use for the evangelist and that sort who rant around; I don't mind their warming up some, but this stamping and shouting does no good."

"People come out in crowds for it," I suggested.

" Yes," he said with a shrug, " but how long does it last? That's the question. Now you take the Salvation Army; *they* keep looking after their converts."

It is this honest desire for what is called in the Western dialect "the real thing" that is the chief impulse of the insurgents against convention in all its forms. Certain forms of conventionality are of course necessary whenever men act in concert. Conformity to tactical regulations can never cease to be essential to the efficiency of an army; but ultimately it is efficiency, not conformity to tactics, that saves an army from being a mere military organization. So some form of worship and of polity is essential to the efficiency of a church; but it is efficiency that saves a church from being a mere ecclesiastical organization. The revolt against conventionality in religious life as I noted it in the Middle West was not against forms and ceremonies as such, but against that conventionalism, whether in ceremony or belief or conduct, which is substituted for "the real thing." And this revolt is by no means confined to the territory of the Church. The "keen business Christian," who has "tact, push, and principle," is losing his hold on many of the Western Young Men's Christian Associations. A Sunday afternoon service, such as I attended in an Iowa city, devoted wholly, except for the hymns, to addresses and prayers about raising money for a debt, is not quite so characteristic of a Western Association as it once was. In the work of the Associated Charities and similar societies the revolt against conventionalism is very marked. Some statements made to me by an officer of a charitable organization in that Iowa city may illustrate how practical that revolt is:

"Until recently there was an annual charity ball given in the city. Now that that has been given up, we have better relations with all sorts of people, and charitable work has less perfunctory and more real support. Nevertheless, there are people who donate to churches and colleges, and yet gouge their washerwomen and underpay their coachmen. It was discovered, for instance, that one wealthy woman, who gave to charity, was paying fifty cents a dozen for the hemming of napkins. Awhile ago a man telephoned to our office asking for relief for a poor woman. The society made an investigation, and discovered immediately that this man was in debt to the woman! As soon as he found out that some one was interested in her rights, he paid up half his debt and will pay the other half. On the other hand, a certain working-girl became acquainted with a needy woman with several children. She persuaded the woman to share a room with her ' on halves,' and began to learn ' fancy washing ' with her. They soon became adept, and as there is a great demand for that kind of work well done, they had a fairly comfortable income before long. That girl *gave* nothing, but *did* something. That is the kind of charitable work we are interested in."

If the churches are the last to feel the effect of this revolt from conventionalism, it is because conventionalism finds its strongest hold in the minds of the rank and file in the churches. The clergyman in the Middle West more than anywhere else, unless it is in the remoter quarters of

New England, is required by a public opinion, which he could not withstand if he would, to conform to certain standards of thought (or at least public expression) and of conduct which his congregation set up for him. Under this tacit supervision many of the clergymen, especially among the younger men, are more restive than they like to admit. The more conscientious a young minister is, the more he objects to have people who are certainly no more thoughtful and no better trained than he designate what his mental processes should be; and the more he also objects to have people who are certainly no more morally responsible than he decide just what things are right and wrong for him to do. Consequently there is a certain proportion of ministers who are in sympathy with the revolt against religious conventionalism. It so happened that the men that I met who were keenly alive to the spirit of revolt were mainly, on the one hand, men outside the Church, and, on the other hand, ministers. The one man who was an indubitable exception was the clerk of a church which had caught the spirit of revolt from the stimulating personality of its minister. Such a church, however, is an exception, because such a minister is rare. Most of the insurgents, as I saw them, were, therefore, either the so-called "unchurched" or ministers at the mercy of their congregations.

This explains the experience of a young clergyman as he told it to me. He had been in charge of a church in one of the Dakotas. In that region conventionalism has not yet obtained the sway it has in more settled regions. Although the members of the church were conventional enough, they depended for the support of the church to some degree upon the community at large. The minister was therefore measurably his own master in thought and conduct. As a result his experience proved to him that his steadiest support, both moral and material, came from men who were members of no church. The result to the active religious life of his church was highly beneficial. Circumstances like these, however, which enable the two extreme classes of insurgents to join forces to increase genuine religious life, are very uncommon, and in the Middle West almost impossible.

Ministers who have the impulse to be outspoken in their revolt against convention may be roughly divided into four categories, according to the way in which they yield to that impulse — or resist it. Into one class may be put those who through circumstance, or more likely their own tactlessness, find themselves adrift. Some of these go into other professions. I was told by one man, himself an ex-minister, who was promoting a new "fraternal benefit order," that he had received forty applications for appointment to agencies from ministers alone. Others, who can be said to form the second category, preferring to remain in the pastorate, restrain their tendency to outspokenness, become conformists in order to secure support for their families, and as they lose their genuineness gradually cease to chafe under their limitations. Occasionally may be found a minister who belongs by right to a third category — one who proves strong enough, and forgets himself sufficiently, to go to work, without domineering, for the education of his people in the wholesome hatred of shams. I met one such minister, but he did not live in the real domain of conventional religion. Any young minister with courage and without egotism might find it a high and yet reasonable ambition to achieve a place among men of this third category. There are, however, in a fourth category, some ministers who, choosing to remain in the pastorate as the best place in which to fight the battle for reality in religion, accept the risk of being adrift most of the time, face the obloquy which is visited upon ministers who are "without charge," and then proceed to be themselves, rather than try to be their deacons or pew-holders, in what they think and do. Naturally, they have egotism as well as courage.

It was my good fortune to spend some time in the company of a minister who had this spirit of willingness to face the consequences of his convictions. Though not one of those ministers who by virtue of exceptional strength and self-forgetfulness become real leaders, he was representative of a certain class of men who by their outspokenness are doing much to cast discredit upon the spirit of religious conventionality. At the time I met him he was pastor of a Congregational church in a small Iowa town. He was a big, broad-shouldered man, who showed the vigor and frankness of his character in every movement. I wish I could reproduce the impression of candor and facile strength that he gave as he talked, not so much of himself or his work as of the people in the places where he had lived and their conditions of life. On the way to his town of T——, I spoke of the country through which we were passing.

"Most of the farms are occupied by tenants who hire their laborers. The Iowa farm-hand works six weeks in the spring and then six weeks more later in the year, and then is 'fired' — about the most unsatisfactory life possible. Within my memory the Iowa farm-tenant has developed much like the Irish tenant. The farmers of a generation ago made their money and then moved to town. These retired farmers are niggardly — they've gotten into penurious habits — and they don't do any good to the towns they live in. Then they rent their farms to poorer men, and require full payment. The existence of these absentee landlords means a lot of poor devils just scraping along. I know one man who at the end of the year didn't have enough corn to feed his team, and yet he had a binful which he couldn't touch. That man hates everybody and has no use for religion."

"What shall *we* do?" said a friend of mine who was traveling with us. "What will the seer say?"

"That's the question. It is simple: adopt some just way of renting land to the man who uses it, and some way of taking the railroads

out of the hands of those who have a private
snap. I'm a landlord myself. I was raised as
a plutocrat, and was taught that my father
owned all outdoors. I clerked in a country
store (what is called nowadays a 'department
store' — sold everything), and when I went into
the ministry I thought that the labor agitation
was simply the growl of unsuccessful men
against success. Here " — the train was drawing up to a station — " is a typical railroad
town. The railroad company has made a real-
estate thing of it. This division is a hundred
and forty-four miles. Terrible! Some crews
work sixty hours at a stretch. I buried a man
who worked for fifty hours straight on a pile-
driver; he lost his hold and fell into the river.
Here there's one church that is trying to divide
railroad men into classes. Railroads are perfectly willing to have their men form brother-
hoods, for they pull apart. Firemen are just
waiting for a strike of engineers, for then they'll
go in and run the trains."

After some interesting, but for the purpose
of this article irrelevant, discussion of labor
questions, our conversation was guided, by some
questions I asked, into consideration of some of
this man's experiences. After giving an ac-

count of his pastorate in a church which had, when he went to it, only two women as members, and in a year and a half grew to have a membership of seventeen, he told of his going to the city of C——.

"It was just after the panic," he explained, "and the Congregational church asked me to come. I was the only 'cheap boy' they could find. It was really a railroad men's church. The railroads at that time introduced a bill into the Legislature providing for 'benefits'—a scheme to make employees pay damages for accidents occurring to them. An amendment to frustrate that scheme was introduced, and I went down to lobby for it. The railroad men hailed me with delight as the one minister who would help. But when I was asked by some of the railroad men to stand for their political party, I told them I wouldn't have anything to do with a rotten institution. That's why I left the church. I made a mistake in that; for my successor, though a good man, wasn't in touch with the railroad men. I think some day I may go back and organize an independent church—not a workingman's church, but a church for all kinds together—for unless the Church has a message for social conditions it had better get off the earth."

"Shall we change conditions," my friend inquired, " or change men? "

"The tunnel is working at both ends," was the laconic answer, in railroad metaphor. "Take a boy of seventeen or eighteen; he naturally has ambitions, not for money or fame, but for some noble ideals; but he gets out into the world and goes for money; for he feels in his conditions the spirit of greed, catches it, and — *There's* a dead town," he said, interrupting himself, as we whizzed by a village whose shaded, grass-bordered streets made it look like a Massachusetts village come West for a visit.

On our arrival at T—— we walked and drove about the town. By the way in which he was accosted, by his familiarity with men of all kinds whom we chanced to meet, by many little incidents, it was easy to see that our host had a very intimate knowledge of the lives and characters of the people in this community. Here, he pointed out, was a house where there lived a man who got so much a week and had to pay such and such rent; there was the home of a poor family, in which a child died and no one offered to help except the keeper of an illegal dive across the street, perhaps for business reasons; that house back from the street was

occupied by an absentee landlord; this little
white house with the board walk in front was
the home of a humble, devout old couple with a
lot of money laid by — the old man was in the
habit of secretly doing a great deal of good
with his money in very wise ways, some of
which our host specified; along that side of the
town was the poor quarter — a good many
foreigners, mostly Catholics, almost every house
suggesting some human story. So our tour
continued until we bade farewell to our host.

His burly frame, his cheerful, clean-shaven
face, and his paternal relations with the people
invited the priestly appellation, "Father."
That made it seem appropriate that he should
still be popularly known by his college nickname,
"Pa." When we had left, my friend, who is
himself a minister, and whose judgment is always sane and well considered, turned to me
and said: "Remember,'Pa' is full of his ideas,
but there are old people who are living their
faith with just as much sincerity as he has, and
they haven't his appreciation of social conditions. The old man is always talking about
the condition of his soul, keeping near to Christ,
and conversion; but A and B [naming two
young men of our acquaintance] are talking

about this life, and whether there is justice or injustice, and how we can cure certain evils. In prayer-meeting the old want to have ' testimonies,' the young want to discuss social problems. The minister to-day needs to be broad enough to feel both sides of the truth—broader than ever."

The last time I saw our vigorous host, the rather quixotic free-lance against all conventionalism, was at a meeting of an association of churches. He was called upon to make a report of his church, and he made it in characteristic disregard of possible consequent reflections upon himself. He began by a reference to the conditions of life in the town; then described the young people's society, which was fairly active when he became pastor. " But now," he continued, "it is dead and only lacks burial. There are two women's societies; one is a Woman's Working Society that does no work — except to raise money. The other is the Woman's Missionary Society. It is divided into twelve bands. Each band makes a clean sweep of the town every month. Every new family gets twelve invitations during the year — one a month. The Society's work is entirely independent of the pastor, and goes on whether there is a pastor or not. It is stronger to-day than ever. It is remarkable in organization and in spirit. You see, I'm reporting, not about the pastor, but about the church. As to the Sunday-school —" " Time's up," interrupted the moderator. " Oh, I can quit any time," he replied. " We've got a church over there. Come over and see it."

It would be a mistake to infer from the independence of this particular religious free-lance that the revolt against conventionalism is in general essentially quixotic. He was rather a striking example in one direction (the sociological) of a tendency that I felt was evident, though less marked, among many ministers in many directions, sociological, theological, ecclesiastical, and ethical. And this tendency has a very real bearing upon practical religious work. How true this is I learned specifically from a young man who was carrying on a mission in one of the cities of the Middle West. He had been a wandering " street fakir " until some happening suddenly brought him to the determination to turn his life into the direction of decency and usefulness. To one minister after another he went for moral backing, but each in turn had only some conventional phrase to

offer — sound enough, in the orthodox sense,
Scriptural, he acknowledged, but somehow not
very vital, not very real to him. At last one
minister started him on the way to getting the
strength and courage that he needed, and enabled him to turn his determination into action.
He broke with his old way of living, and at
once, without money, almost without friends,
undertook as his life-work to help others out
of degradation into self-respect and right living. He had no special theology, but he did
have a faith in the power that had made a different man of him. He had also a practical
acquaintance with the sort of people he wanted
to help. He knew their dissatisfaction with
their life, for he had shared that with them; he
knew also their pretense about enjoying life,
for he had shared that too. But he was distrustful of himself — he was not good enough,
so he imagined, to help them. So he undertook to provide assistance to the needy, establish a place of meeting, and get an audience,
but instead of publicly speaking himself, he
turned to the ministers of the city to bring to
the people the message of power. Then again
he was disappointed. Not that any refused to
respond to his request, but most of them had

no message that meant anything to these people.   It was again the conventional phrase instead of the real vital word.   Still he persisted;
he did not alter his plan of calling upon the
ministers because of disappointment at first.
And for his persistence he was rewarded.
Brought into acquaintance with men and women who were grievously and consciously in
need of moral help, ministers who had begun
by saying merely the conventional things
learned to be genuine and real before that audience.   As a consequence, that one man with
his rescue mission has, without knowing it,
done more to break down religious conventionalism than any other force in the city.   And
yet there are strongholds of conventionalism
which he found impregnable.   The most impregnable were in two churches, one representative of the most wealthy and cultivated
classes in the city, the other made up distinctively of the ignorant, though fairly well-to-do,
and shepherded by an uneducated minister of
the literalist type.   The minister of the wealthy
church had responded with the greatest kindness to the request of the superintendent of the
mission, but, after a number of experiences, said
to him at last, " There is nothing I should care

so much to do as to be able to speak to the people of the mission, but I find I cannot — I do not know how; I must acknowledge my limitations. Financial help, however, our church can and will give you." The uneducated minister took quite the reverse attitude; he not only responded to requests, but volunteered his services as a speaker; he shouted, gesticulated, reiterated his shibboleths; but all to no purpose. His failure was profound. And yet he continued to embarrass the superintendent with his proffers of service, until he developed into a permanent problem. On the other hand, the superintendent spoke in terms of gratitude with regard to the religious influence upon the people of the mission exerted by certain of the ministers of the city. One of these ministers I have already referred to, in connection with another incident, as by nature above the understanding of the conformist. The story of this superintendent, as I learned it partly from himself and partly from others, was one of the most cheering evidences of the degree to which the revolt against convention has already extended in the Middle West.

No reaction against an evil is always wholly good. The reaction against the spirit of conformity has its perversions. In some cases it has become attenuated into a rather frothy sentiment. One young preacher, very popular if judged by the crowds that come to his meetings, who is a leader in an "independent movement," graciously gave me a few moments of his very busy life; but I got little from him except some vague generalities about hurting nobody's conscience, about the insufficiency of religious work through accessions of converts to the churches, and about the need of making "a direct assault upon public opinion." On the other hand, this revolt has in some cases hardened into purely ethical experiments. At Hull House, Chicago, for instance, where such courageous and triumphant work for civic and social decency has been done, an incidental mention which I made of a possible religious basis for such work was met with a chilling disclaimer of any trace of religious motive in their efforts, the more chilling because in strong contrast to the cordial welcome I personally received.

And yet every independent church movement is by no means therefore sentimental. A great theater service I attended in Chicago was sustained by a vast work of practical beneficence. Nor does every social settlement feel the religious motive alien to its life, as was abundantly proved even in a very brief visit I made to Chicago Commons; for it so happened that on that visit I found the evening service of a neighborhood church being held in the modern and beautiful building erected and maintained by the Commons. Indeed, even those phases of the reaction against conventionalism that seem most unfortunate are signs of hopefulness, after all; for they add to the multiform assaults that are being made upon the deadening spirit of religious pretense, and hasten the day of its overthrow.

THE LEAVEN AND THE LUMP

XI

THE LEAVEN AND THE LUMP

ALMOST all Americans are of course essentially Europeans transplanted. A good deal of what we like to call distinctively American is composed of traits characteristic of Europe in the seventeenth or eighteenth century.[1] There is reason, therefore, in distinguishing between Asiatic and European immigrants, whether we consider them as social, economic, political, or religious factors in the life of the Nation. There is reason even in raising the query whether the African people who have been on this continent for generations are not more truly aliens than the newcomers from the countries of Europe. At any rate, it is fair to say that most of the foreigners who

[1] Mr. Barrett Wendell has drawn an interesting parallel between the Yankee and the seventeenth-century Briton in his "Literary History of America."

are streaming in to make their homes here are meeting not with an utterly strange civilization, but rather with a different phase of the same civilization to which they have been accustomed. To this as well as to the American spirit of religious toleration I attribute the fact that nowhere in the course of my trip did I meet with evidence that newly arrived Europeans had found occasion after their arrival for any violent readjustment of their religious life. Whatever adjustment came to my attention was invariably the result of a comparatively slow process.

Such adjustment, moreover, was not by any means all on one side. The process of making the Nation is not the simple one, as every one knows, of turning Irishmen and Germans and Swedes into Yankees; it is, so to speak, chemical, and the result is neither the one element nor the other, but a new substance. The immigrants are not being modified without modifying America in return. The making of America did not end with the adoption of the Constitution. It is only necessary to cite the history of music in America for the last generation to suggest how much the Europeans who have come into the United States within that time have contributed to the national character.

Similarly in religious life there was not a little that I observed which could have come from no other source than these people whom we are accustomed to regard as being "assimilated" like so much food.

As I came across foreigners in various parts of the country three questions were in my mind: First, in what ways is the immigrant population affecting religious life in America? Second, in what ways is America affecting religious life in the immigrant population? Third, what are churches, or other religious bodies, or individual Christians doing to use religion for the purpose of making out of these immigrants loyal American citizens?

In order to find definite answers to these questions, one ought to be able to use with some fluency the languages of these foreigners, and ought to know their lives far more intimately than the casual observer can possibly know them. It is hardly necessary to say that I shall attempt no definite answers. I shall simply record my experiences as they touched upon foreign people in America, using the three questions as interpreters.

It is perfectly evident to any one with eyes in his head who travels in the United States that there are many communities of foreigners which contribute little but their numbers to the Nation, and receive in return little more than a space in which to live. In religious life they have only such significance as springs from isolation. Such were the Bohemians that I saw in Virginia. They had settled in the Dakotas, I was told, but had been frozen out by the long winters, and had sought a milder climate not far from Petersburg. I could well believe the old-time Southern gentleman who said to me that they "refused to affiliate with the inhabitants." Their mobility was evidence of their unwillingness to mingle with strangers. "They keep great mastiffs," continued my informant, "which scare people off; they refuse to speak English; they won't work with other people, though you can see them at work on the roads; they are Catholics and won't have anything to do with Lutherans, even of their own blood; they level abandoned graveyards, using the gravestones for landmarks. I have even seen in one kitchen a stone, used to make bread on, with the inscription, 'Sacred to the memory of ——.' They drive out the 'niggroes'; that," he added as his opinion, "is the only good thing they do."

In the big cities there are colonies of foreigners, as is well known, who are almost if not quite as isolated as these Bohemians of Virginia. A resident in a social settlement situated among Italians in the city of New York told me that he knew of Italian and Sicilian villages which he had visited from which half the population had gone bodily to the neighborhood of his social settlement or to other places in the American metropolis. Such transplanted communities retained in the New World their old local customs, their religious peculiarities, their neighborhood acquaintances; indeed, were almost as sufficient unto themselves as they were in their Italian or Sicilian homes.

Such " side-tracked communities," as they have been called, exist in all parts of the country. Some of them count their age by generations. Particularly is this true in the State of Pennsylvania. Many of the so-called Pennsylvania Dutch are nearly as far out of the current of present-day American life as they ever were. With some of these, whose ancestors were American born, I have found it almost as hard to communicate in English as if they had just landed from Germany. Under these conditions the persistence of secluded churches and sects is but natural: the Wine-brennerians and the Dunkards, for instance, with their exotic rites, the Moravians with their very beautiful customs and unworldly spirit, the Little Russians, nominally under the con-trol of Roman Catholic archbishops, but retain-ing, as in Galicia and Hungary, their Slavonic liturgy and their distinctive forms of saint-worship. Such religious bodies, interesting, picturesque, and, in the case of the Moravians, valuable as they are, may be said to be only incidental to the religious life of America.

As a rule, however, I found a process of action and reaction going on between the for-eign people and the communities in which they had settled. The most evident result of such a process is a change in the religious life of the native American population. Sometimes this change is one of decline and can be traced in large measure to the exclusiveness of the for-eigners. A town in southern Illinois which I visited, for example, has been for decades sub-ject to gradual inroads of Germans and Bohe-mians. In the early days of the town it had been, according to my informant, "historic ground for Methodism." Now it is filled with

Catholics, Evangelicals, Lutherans, and German Methodists. These foreigners were used in the old countries to a life of drudgery, and they retained their habits of unremittent toil in their new surroundings. The Bohemians often made their working days last from three o'clock in the morning to nine o'clock at night. The American farmers could not — or would not — stand such a pace, and consequently yielded the land to the newcomers. The result has been a gradual but irresistible diminishing of English-speaking congregations and a spirit of lethargy among the English-speaking people who remain. A contributive force in this process has been the tendency, which exists in the Middle West to only a less degree than in New England, of the more enterprising spirits in the villages and smaller towns to seek the supposed advantages offered by the rapid growth of cities. The decay of religious institutions has been accompanied by a weakening of the moral character of the community, indicated not so much by the increase of vice or crime as by the paralysis of the will and the obliteration of the spirit of hopefulness and self-reliance.

Another effect of the presence of Europeans

in an American community is to be seen in the
result of their example in altering the publicly
accepted standards of moral conduct. Whether
these standards are as a rule conventional or
vital depends upon one's point of view. One
minister whom I met in Kansas considered
them vital. He had formerly been the pastor
of a church in St. Louis. Many of his parishioners were Germans who did not have his
views about the delusive qualities of beer, or
the proper ways of observing the Lord's day.
He told me that one of his trustees who was
fond of taking his family out driving on Sunday mornings would not infrequently remark
if they happened to meet on Saturday: "Vell,
looks like to-morrow be stormy; I'll be at
church." The minister confessed that he was
glad to flee into Kansas from such a demoralizing foreign influence. In another and even
more distinctively German city I met a minister
who testified to a somewhat similar result of
foreign influence, though he had an altogether
different opinion of it.

"When I first came here," he told me, "I
was fresh from New England, and I had my
New England ideas about right and wrong. I
soon discovered that the Puritan feeling is

dissipated here. A deacon — he was not a German — drove me about to show me the city. We came to a big brewery.

" 'There are three grades of beer brewed there,' he said.

" 'Is there any real difference?' I inquired, for I wanted to know all that I could about the industries of the city in which I was to live.

" 'Yes, indeed; there is a very decided difference,' he answered.

" 'Which is considered the best?' I asked.

" ' 'Well,' he said in reply, 'for *my* part *I* like " export " best'; then seeing the surprise in my face, and anticipating my next and rather personal question, he added, ' Oh, yes, I *do*.' "

This clergyman, though pastor of a church strictly Puritan by right of descent, had come to believe that the influence of the foreign element upon the moral standard of the churches was wholesome; he believed that it revealed the conventionality of those standards, and that the churches' conception of Christian character could and ought to be freed from bondage to mere conventionality; or, in other words, that it introduced perspective into the Chinese flatness by which the Puritan depicted all acts of which he approved as of equal moral value.

So much for the influence of immigrants upon the religious life of America. What, in turn, has been the influence of the American democracy upon the religious life of these immigrants? In many respects this is a harder question to answer than the former, because it is harder for an American to trace changes in the life of an alien people than in the life of people among whom he lives. Nevertheless, some of these changes are very obvious. The American system of public education very rapidly breaks down racial barriers between children of different nationalities, and therefore modifies religious life in those respects in which it is determined by racial custom. An Irish priest pointed out to me the distinction that lies between German Catholics and Irish Catholics. In Germany, he said, the people are supremely proud of their church; they are ambitious to have the building well constructed and beautiful, the altar properly adorned, and the establishment well taken care of; but their relations to their priest are formal and somewhat impersonal. The Irish, on the other hand, are proverbially careless, not to say slovenly, in their care of the church; they are willing to have it and all its appurtenances 'shabby; but with their priest they are on intimate terms; they love to have him come as a familiar friend into their homes, be they poor or rich; they turn to him in every need — when they are harassed by debt they want his legal advice; when they are sick they look upon his presence as medicine; at their festivities he is the honored guest; and at the approach of death he is more than the official of the church, he is the companion for a little way on the road to the region of the blest.   When the Germans come to this country they bring their loyalty to their church, and they build fine buildings for consecration.   When the Irish become American they retain their loyalty to their priest and keep him as their friend.   The German children and Irish children, however, play together, go to school together, speak the same language, and exchange ideas.   Before long the Germans begin to be infected with the Irish loyalty to the priest, while they find their pride in their church in no wise impaired.   The Irish, too, learn from the Germans; they still are as fond as ever of their Father Foley or their Father O'Brien, but they begin to be ashamed of their church buildings, that are so shabby beside the German churches, and they make them more tidy and try to improve them, and finally decide to rebuild. This Irish priest told me that he had gone West gradually, and he said that you could see the difference in the Irish people on each stage toward the setting sun, until when you came to Iowa, say, they were new creatures entirely. Before I bade him good-by he said to me — and he knew I was a Protestant — "We're like the islands of the sea; separate on top, but joined together down below the water."

A German Methodist of the Middle West talked to me very frankly about the people of his nationality. Most of what he said I found elsewhere confirmed. Some of his conversation with me, so far as it bears on this question of American influence upon the religious life of immigrants, is worth quoting.

"About thirty per cent., I should say, of German immigrants," was his statement, "keep up their connections with the established churches — those are the Lutheran and the Reformed. The majority of these you would find difficult to distinguish from Catholics; they only go to their churches occasionally, and then not out of individual conviction — more out of custom and conformity. Most German immigrants keep away from the established churches because they are among the things for which they left Germany. It is very hard to work among such Germans, because of their rationalistic tendencies and conservatism."

" Both rationalistic and conservative? What do you mean? "

" I mean that Germans stick to their views, whatever they are. They are not enthusiastic, especially in religion. Germans can be enthusiastic in politics — but not in religion. So the churches in this country that are made up of such people not in the established churches are liberal. In Germany such people would belong to free (that is, irreligious) societies; here many of them, being free from the prejudice that they would have in Germany, belong to churches. These churches have had an influence on the Lutheran Church, and consequently the German churches in America are more liberal than they are in Germany. For the same reason the Lutherans are more ' spiritual ' here than there. Many Lutheran churches have but one service; but if a German Methodist church is near by they need to keep up services to save their own people to themselves. The tendency in German churches in America is toward a liberal theology (though not the 'New Theology,' which is rationalistic though religious. The New Theology will appeal to the better educated of the German rationalists). In the East the German churches are becoming too much Americanized."

" Why do you think so? " I inquired.

" Because when Germans become Americanized they ought to go to American, not German, churches. The German churches ought to be kept for those who want to go to church where German is used. There are a good many Germans who use English in business and even in their families who will not have use for English sermons. That is because they think of their religion in the German-Bible-language."

This conservatism in the use of language I noticed as a force frequently destructive of foreign churches in America. The older generation holds on to the use of the native tongue; in the meantime the younger people, who find English, to which they have become accustomed in the school, on the street, in business, and even in their homes, more acceptable, go to other churches; then when the older generation dies, the church dies, too. This has been the history of the Huguenot churches in

America — of which only one, and that now wholly using English, is left; it will probably be the history of many other churches. So the foreign streams empty into the American sea.

In just two places I found some answer to the question: Are churches or individual Christians using the religious motive as a force for making out of these foreigners citizens in sympathy with the principles of the Republic and appreciative of its gifts? In other words, to what extent among these foreigners is religion made a cause of patriotism? In both cases where I found an answer it happened that the foreigners were not Europeans; in one case they were American Indians, in the other Armenians and Chinese. Without question these two instances are representative of many; but I cite them to show not so much what is being done as what might be.

In Kansas there is a school for Indians carried on by the United States Government. The principal, a man whose stalwart character was well expressed in a physique and bearing that were emphatically vigorous, had the kindness to give me a glimpse of the school and its work. Strong, clean work it was — that I could see in the shops and in the bearing of the students. It was, however, the religious element in the school that seemed to me most significant. The principal's sympathetic appreciation of the religious instincts of the Indian was very keen, and to those instincts he appealed with a most practical tact. "Our discipline here is military," he said, "and therefore we have always had a guard-house for offenders, and it has been in frequent — sometimes daily — use; but discipline here is not merely for the sake of maintaining order — it is supremely for the sake of inculcating the love of order. So I decided upon a new method of discipline. When our chapel was built we designed it so as to include in the lower story a gymnasium. I want our students to associate religion with healthfulness and vigor of mind and body. When the building was ready for use I called the students together and I said to them: 'Boys, to-day we open the gymnasium for the first time. At the same time to-day I am going to close the guard-house, I hope for the last time.' The guard-house has not been used once since then, and that was months ago." That is one instance in which I saw religion used as a force in preparing aliens for citizenship.

The other instance was in a New England city. Involving more didactic effort than the case I have just described, this illustration was somewhat more pronounced. An active member of a large Congregational church in this city had been for years interested in the foreigners that had drifted into the services. One day, while he was teaching a men's class in the Sunday-school, an Armenian presented himself as a pupil. The Armenian was looking for help in learning English and in finding support. In the course of a few weeks other Armenians joined him. Before long the teacher had to abandon his former class and give all his time to the Armenians. "I told them," he said, "that if they would come regularly, I would teach them English and help them to become good Americans. So they came, and this is what I kept saying to them : ' You Armenians find freedom here and a chance to live and be useful. You call this " God's country " and you are right. It is God that has made this country what it is. So since this is God's country you all ought to be brothers!' One day a Chinaman appeared at the Sunday-school, and the officers of the school, not knowing what else to do with him, sent him in to me. After the session the Armenians came up to me and protested against having a 'foreigner' like him admitted. 'Look here,' said I, 'when you Armenians came didn't I put up with you? Then I guess you Armenians must stand the Chinaman. Didn't I say that this is God's country because he has made us all to be brothers to one another?' So the Chinaman remained and other Chinese came. One day a Chinaman whom I knew to be honest and orderly was tormented by small boys, there was some disorder, and the Chinaman was put into jail. I immediately bailed him out. Thereupon an Armenian who had been constantly asking for financial assistance came to me and said, 'You help the Chinaman: why don't you help me?' That's the failing of these Armenians, to be begging for help. I said to him, 'I didn't do anything for the Chinaman that I wouldn't do for an American; and I won't do anything for you that I wouldn't do for an American. This is God's country because God has put people here on their own reliance.' So it has gone. The Armenians have organized an Armenian Congregational church, and they worship here in the lecture-room. As the older people pass away the church will disintegrate, for the younger Armenians prefer to use English and unite with the American church; and it is better so.   These American flags and streamers that are decorating their room were put up for the Christmas celebration; they chose the Stars and Stripes instead of evergreens because they are beginning to see now that Christianity is helping them to become good Americans."

It is plain that the Republic and its foreign population are leaven and lump in turns.   My general impression may be briefly stated in this wise: The effect of America upon the religious life of immigrants is almost uniformly wholesome; the influence of immigrants upon American religious life, though sometimes temporarily demoralizing, is, on the whole, decidedly in the direction of breadth and genuineness.

NEW SECTS AND OLD

XII

NEW SECTS AND OLD

AMONG the most interesting religious bodies in the United States I should count the so-called fraternal insurance organizations. Strictly, these are not sects, of course, yet they have many characteristics that give them a resemblance to denominational bodies. Indeed, each of the most important marks of distinction which exclude them from being popularly classed among the sects — that they disclaim all connection with the Church, that no denomination "fellowships" them, that they have no order of clergy, and that they do not usually hold their stated meetings on Sunday—can with equal truth be attributed to some Christian denomination. On the other hand, almost all of them have a more or less avowedly religious basis. Some of them are nominally theocratic,

285

each having its own epithet, appropriate to its general nomenclature, which it applies to God. The order which does not place belief in deity and in immortality among its principles is exceptional. Possibly this is because insurance and relief, which it is the object of such associations to promote, center about the fact of death. Like the religious impulse, the ethical idea of the Church and the fraternities is largely identical in terms, even to the cant title "brother."

More obvious resemblances to religious denominations, however, have come from the adoption or imitation by the orders of what in the Church are called "the means of grace"— the Bible, common worship, and personal piety. The promoter of one of these orders, for instance, told me that he began by selecting a book as a basis. More's "Utopia" was his choice. Then he prepared a ritual, formulated according to the ideas and in the very phraseology of the book. Wherever now that order has spread—chiefly in the Middle West—there are men whose feeling toward More's "Utopia" might be described not inaptly as personal devotion. Other orders have their own scriptures, their own rituals, and their own brands of piety.

"In fact," the disciple of More said, with a smile, after describing an organization named and patterned in accordance with one of Scott's novels, "it is not uncommon for members to be heard saying, 'I mean to read my Ivanhoe more!' or, 'If we only lived up to our ritual!'— just like a woman in a prayer-meeting!"

The real religious significance of these orders seemed to me strangely overlooked by most of the church people with whom I talked on the subject in various parts of the country. As a rule, it seemed, according to their view, to consist in the degree in which these orders competed or coöperated with the churches. In one place I would be told that for many men they took the place of the churches — as the real guides of moral conduct, inculcating a sort of remunerative altruism; the real teachers of religion, inculcating in place of faith a vague belief in the existence and benevolence of God; and the real leaders of worship, supplanting the clergyman even in the ministrations for the dead. In another place, on the contrary, I would be told that they made deeper the ethical teaching of the Church, reinforced its religious influence, and coöperated with it in public worship. The more fundamental significance of fraternal organizations, as I learned of them, certainly quite irrespective of locality, may be stated as threefold.   First, they show that men, when left quite free of any ecclesiastical direction, are still strongly governed by religious conceptions, however vague and undeveloped. Second, they illustrate how widespread and spontaneous is the impulse to express religious and ethical ideas by ritual, however crude and artificial. Third, they express concretely, though in a rather one-sided and selfish form, that social consciousness which has too often been left by the churches without any other religious or ethical expression.   In one respect, however, these orders are fundamentally distinct from what are commonly accepted as religious bodies: in no case that I heard of did any of these orders proffer a " salvation religion," or furnish any sign even that its religion had anything to do with the failure involved in wrongdoing.   This is perhaps the reason why these orders are not, as it is a most unanswerable argument why they should not be, accepted as substitutes for the Church.   Nevertheless, even when they are not taken too seriously, they constitute an interesting and, in the Middle

West especially, a not inconsiderable phase of religious life in America.

Distinctively ecclesiastical bodies have become so numerous in the United States that the mere brief mention of each of those I chanced to meet with during my journey would require an article by itself wholly encyclopedic in character. The most depressing impression I received, as the result of my trip, was caused by hearing the claim of one sect after another to be the most truly representative of the real Christianity of Jesus and the Apostles. By meeting in person and in somewhat rapid succession, as I did, actual representatives of many different theologies, I heard, as it were, the clamor of creeds, and saw the bewildering confusion of sects that has been the result, under the conditions of absolute religious freedom peculiar to America, of the popular Protestant conviction that salvation depends upon the acceptance of correct dogmas. Of the sects that came to my knowledge there are two distinct and opposite types. One depends for its existence upon the identification of Christianity with some invented or resuscitated doctrine or body of doctrines; the other depends for its existence upon inheritance from historic religious movements. Almost every religious body that belongs in this second classification originated either from a protest against some prevailing error or from some need for the assertion of an inadequately recognized truth. In almost every case the conditions under which the denomination originated have to a great extent disappeared (usually because of the service it has rendered) and the denomination itself now continues chiefly as a witness to a past achievement. Once people affiliated themselves with one or another of these denominations out of conviction; now they belong largely for reasons of personal convenience or family tradition. Of these two types—one recent, the other historic—the former is illustrated by Christian Science, the Christian Catholic Church in Zion, and the Reorganized Church of Latter-Day Saints; the latter, in most emphatic contrast, is illustrated by the Friends and the Moravians.

In view of the rapid spread of Christian Science, it was somewhat surprising to me that I made the acquaintance of only a single votary of Mrs. Eddy's cult, and that was in Maine, on the first day of my trip. I could easily have met others, I suppose, if I had cared to search for them by invading any of the numerous Christian Science Reading-Rooms which I saw in most of the cities I visited; but I did not think it worth while to pick up at haphazard statements concerning the tenets of a sect that has been so assiduous in giving to those tenets currency. I found it more interesting to learn what people not adherents thought about it. Indeed, on several occasions I discovered that the easiest way of approaching the general topic of religious life was by introducing into conversation the specific subject of Christian Science. Everybody seemed to have some experience with regard to it, or some opinion concerning it. The little group of commercial travelers I fell in with in a South Carolina hotel were all mightily interested in the tales of healing that they told one another out of their own fund of experience, and were perfectly frank in admitting that they were readier to concede the claims of a Church that made its chief business to do away with disease and suffering than the claims of churches that made their chief business to preach at people. A journalist of Missouri remarked to me in the course of conversation: "The churches are weaker than they used to be, except the Roman Catholic Church (which I don't understand) and Christian Science. The latter seems to appeal to men especially. This is partly because of the concreteness of its appeal "— a leg healed here, a specific disease cured there — "but its real power lies in the fact that it makes no distinction between hearing the word and doing it "; in other words, that it not only accepts on their face value the promises of Christ that his disciples should be healers of disease as well as he was, but assumes that this function of healing is the very essence of the Gospel itself. Most significant of all were the comments of a physician in Iowa. I asked him if he thought there was anything more in Christian Science than organized and deliberate use of psychological suggestion. "Yes," he replied, " there is a religious principle involved. You will be surprised, perhaps, to know that I have a considerable practice among Christian Scientists. I think that is due mainly to my attempt to avoid antagonism, and to approach their ailments in every case possible from their own point of view. If there is an amputation, I remark, 'You cut your toe-nails, don't you?

Then why not go a little further up and cut off the foot?' Or if there is need for surgical dressings, I inquire if they do not use soap; and then ask, 'Why not use an antiseptic?' It is easy enough to argue from the other direction, and to inquire why, if they do not use medicine, they should not dispense with food. Their reply is always that the reason lies in the imperfection of the individual mind, not in any defect of the 'science.' They put it all up in the air where you can't get at it; so I accept their theory of the imperfection of the individual mind. In many respects my Christian Science patients are the best I have, aside from the fact that they pay their bills (they've been trained to do that by their 'healers'). In a Christian Science household I do not encounter the flustered state of mind that in other households I have to deal with as well as with the disease. If it is a case of confinement, for instance, when ordinarily there is a great deal of nervousness, in the Christian Science household everything is accepted as natural, as in harmony with the mind of God." In addition to human credulity, which has so often served as a cavalier explanation of any religious phenomena, it was to one or all of these three characteristics of Christian Science — its appeal through the concrete, its identifying its faith with practice, and its effectiveness in producing serenity of mind by the easy method of denying the existence of any cause for disturbance — that non-adherents accounted for its growth.

Divine healing is the special stock in trade of a number of new sects, among them the so-called " Christian Catholic Church in Zion " — an enterprise promoted by a man named Dowie. Chicago, eager if undiscriminating, is the Rome for this pope — the wilderness for this Elijah, this John Baptist, to use his own titles for himself. One Sunday afternoon I went to the building used as headquarters of the new Zion. I was directed to "follow the crowd." As I left the building, a short, corpulent man, with a long gray beard, hurried by me, giving me a searching glance as he passed. I recognized him from his pictures on the placards posted about the city. He drove off in a carriage drawn by a pair of spirited horses driven by a liveried coachman. I made my way on foot to the " tabernacle," and entered among a throng of ordinary-looking people. At the farther end of the " tabernacle," back of the platform, were tiers of seats, like those for a chorus in a concert hall, in the midst of which was a reed organ. On the walls were hung trophies supposed to have been obtained from converts, and displayed as tokens of their release from their ills and superstitions: in one place a design composed of crutches; in another the word " drugs " spelled out in empty medicine-bottles; in another a decoration consisting of rosaries and Roman Catholic charms; in another a sort of tapestry made of insurance orders' certificates; and in yet another a cross formed by hot-water bags! The body of the house was filled with people, and the semicircular galleries were well occupied. A woman in white vestments was playing a prelude on the organ. Soon the audience rose. Coming up the aisle were children, walking slowly by twos, wearing white vestments and holding open books in their hands; they mounted the steps to the platform, then, separating, filed up from either side into the tiers of seats. The full length of the aisle was filled twice over with children before there appeared a division of young women similarly vested, and with mortar-board caps. As they approached the platform they began to sing " Crown him with many crowns." Then following came a choir of young men in caps and white vestments; after these white-robed ones came, in black gowns and mortar-board caps, first a choir of middle-aged women, then one of middle-aged men. These followed the others up on the platform, but, the tiers of seats being filled, streamed into the front rows of the galleries. At the end of the procession walked the stout, gray-bearded man, now dressed in a black gown with bishop's sleeves and a hood of white, yellow, and purple. When he reached the platform and turned, the music stopped and all the men removed their caps. No theatrical device could have more effectually concentrated attention upon the central personage. He raised his hand dramatically, and in resonant, assertive tones pronounced a benediction. Thereupon began the most wearisome, in some respects the most interesting, and I think the strangest service I ever attended, original not so much in any new feature as in the ingenious combination of features from many sources: the canticles, hymns, and vestments of the Church of England, the priestly dominance of the Roman Catholic Church, the assumption of divine healing of the Christian Scientist, the reference to immersion of the Baptist sects, the exhorting of the Methodist evangelist, and the promise of the theocratic community of the Mormon. The audience seemed to submit with pleasure to the domineering autocracy of their leader. When he gave out the notices, he spent three-quarters of an hour in setting forth the virtues of his various business ventures — the publishing business of Zion, the great Zion excursion, and the subscription for stock in the new Zion city lots.

"Keep the books of Zion for people to look at, but don't lend! The great mass of mankind are great book-keepers. . . . You have great readiness to borrow books, especially when you can buy them yourselves, you wretches! . . . The Zion's Banner will be the news, eliminating the lies that are common in the papers. . . . This will give me a chance to deal with things that I haven't felt justified in dealing with in the Leaves of [Healing, and I shall deal with them, too; I've never been afraid of men. . . . We guarantee no land of the first series after May 31st, and the second series will be higher in price. . . . We have a right to charge the laggards for indolence. . . . Pray for me about this. I don't like to talk this business, but it is my only chance, and this is God's business, isn't it?"

"Yes," came the answer from some thousand throats.

"Prairie schooners are on their way to Zion city. Some are staying on the land. People coming from England, Germany, Australia. In Canada from a little country place twenty are coming. You Chicago people will wake up to find yourselves outside. I'll be rather glad to see you in the outer darkness, weeping and wailing and gnashing your teeth to see the Canadians on the inside. I'm not much of a business man — I'm an innocent—that's what they say. A lady got 'Dr.' Dowie to pray about selling land—and she sold it, not at a loss either, but at a gain! . . . Give your wife half— that is, if she's in Zion; if not, don't give her anything. . . . Overseer Jane Dowie, pray for her. Can I send her a cablegram sending her love?"

"Yes," came the reply from the audience, like a distant roll of thunder, as they held up their hands.

"A young Frenchman in Paris has given up tobacco, wine, swine's-flesh, and gambling. I want you to pray for him."

" Yes."

" Some of these impudent papers say I have a mighty soft place. Huh! When my wife comes, she'll back me up. Now, then! Have you forgotten all I've said already? . . . Next Lord's Day there will be baptism by triune immersion."

This may give an idea of his methods of financing his enterprise. It did not sound much like the ordinary appeal for church or missionary funds.

In his sermon, which he delivered in front of his pulpit with much shouting, stamping, and pounding, he displayed what his followers doubtless interpreted as moral passion, but what sounded much like savagely exuberant delight in the rhetoric descriptive of the evils he denounced.

" . . . Don't talk as if death were good. It is hateful, hellish, king of terrors; it never blesses, but always curses. . . . The false teachings of the apostate churches have led people to think that death is of God. It is from the devil. . . . I plead for love that will overcome lust, life that will overcome death, health that will overcome disease. May God give us that love!"

"Amen," fervently responded the audience.

"Did he love us as himself? *Answer me!*"

"Yes."

"Did he love us better than himself?"

"Yes."

"Then we should love him, and love others better than ourselves. Do you want that love?"

"Yes."

"Then rise and ask for it."

He offered a petition, stopping at the end of each phrase for the people to repeat it after him. During this prayer, as during every other prayer in the service, the demeanor of the congregation was extraordinarily devout.

"Did you mean it?"

"Yes."

"During the recessional hold your hearts in adoration."

The hymn, a long one, was sung five times over before all the chorus (there must have been some two hundred and fifty) disappeared.

When I left, at the end of three hours, a large part of the people were departing; but even then a negro was preparing on the platform the utensils for the Communion service that was to follow. I was glad to get into the

clearer air outside, and, by a brisk walk along
the edge of the lake, to shake off the feeling
of helplessness that seemed to be contagious in
that fold of submissive sheep.

It was also in Chicago that I had a glimpse
of the seamy side of irresponsible religious
Cæsarism. The sign on a building announced
that here was a mission of the Reorganized
Church of Latter-Day Saints. A little girl in
a torn and dirty dress answered my summons.
She conducted me through a bare, dirty hallway to a room upstairs and called for her
mother. A woman, whose hair hung down in
strings on either side of her rather sallow face,
and whose dress was almost as torn and dirty
as the girl's, appeared and asked me what I
wanted. When she learned that I was interested in her religion, the expression of her face
changed from that of vacant weariness to an
earnestness that was almost luminous. For an
hour, it may have been longer, she talked to me
of her faith. She explained how wicked had
been the lapse of the Mormons from the teachings of Joseph Smith; how the remnant of
true believers had been basely defrauded of
their name as the real Church of Latter-Day

Saints; how impossible it was for more than one genuine Church of Christ to exist; and how it happened that, because of the introduction of false revelations in favor of polygamy, the one true Church had been reduced to the body of believers who, forced to call themselves Reorganized, and commonly known as "non-polygamous Mormons," now have their headquarters in Iowa. She expounded the Scriptures to show that triple immersion and laying on of hands, both ordinances only as properly administered, were essential to salvation. She showed me the room in which the services were held, and when I took my departure put into my hands some tracts and leaflets setting forth the doctrines upon which the hope of the world depends. A masterful mind with some ingenuity in constructing dogmas by a new juxtaposition of Scripture texts — that seems to be one element common to all these "new" sects. The other element is furnished by that host of people who like to be mastered because it saves them trouble.

"We believe that the canon of Scripture is not full, but that God, by his Spirit, will continue to reveal his word to man until the end of time." This statement, which is from one of these pamphlets of the "non-polygamous Mormons," represents the crude form of a profoundly religious belief which has never been wholly without voice in the Christian Church. That the Holy Spirit is always directly inspiring the words and the acts of believers was the conviction of the Christians in the Apostolic age, and the distinguishing doctrine of the Montanists. In modern times it has found most adequate expression with the Friends. So wide has been their influence, and so happily has this influence, unpolemically exerted, been reinforced by modern conceptions of the immanence of God, that to-day the idea of the "Inner Light," in fact if not in name, has been accepted among all bodies of Christians. It has even been formulated into harsh creeds of recent manufacture, to do service for some new cult and to justify some Arcana Cœlestia, or Book of Mormon, or Key to the Scriptures. In the meantime, as this belief has become less distinctive of the Friends, it has apparently lost its hold upon them. I tried to discover the reason for this from a Friend minister. He had remarked that the Friends as a body had not accepted the conclusions of the Higher Criticism of the Bible.[1]

" Then they believe in the infallibility of the Bible, and accept it as the ultimate authority? "

" Yes," he said emphatically, " we hold close to the Bible."

" You believe that there is inspiration of men to-day? "

" Yes. Shakespeare and Longfellow were inspired in a sense, but not as the holy men of old."

" How about the holy men of to-day? "

" Yes, they are inspired, we believe, but are capable of error."

" Then the Holy Spirit does not inspire infallibly, as in ancient times? "

He made a reference to the changes in revising the King James Version, the pertinence of which I did not understand, and concluded by saying that the errors were so slight that they occasioned no difficulty. Then, after a discus-

---

[1] Neither this statement concerning " Higher Criticism " nor the preceding one concerning the " Inner Light " is to be considered as universally true of the whole body of Friends. This Friend minister would find other Friends strongly disagreeing with him. Nevertheless his statements are true of certain Friends and represent some existing tendencies which are in thorough accord with the proneness of human nature to substitute the mechanical for the vital.

sion as to the source of authority for the acceptance of the canon, he finally dismissed the
subject by saying, " In the providence of God,
the Bible is here as we find it." The only conclusion to which this conversation could lead
was that the desire for an outward and visible
repository of authority was too strong for a
faith in an Inner Light that was originally less
a dogma than an experience.

Like the Friends, the Moravians seem to find
reason for separate existence as a religious
body, not in doctrinal distinctions, but in historic continuity. So long as there are differences of denomination which make impossible
organic unity of the Christian Church, there is
no better reason for the separate existence of
any religious body than a great history; and
certainly that reason the Moravians abundantly
have. The sign that even this reason is no
longer as effectual as it was is evident in the
waning of some of their customs. Many of
their observances, however — for instance, the
Easter service at dawn in the old burying-
ground, or the announcement of deaths by
chorales played by four trombonists from the
church belfry, the second chorale being always

that designated by custom as appropriate to the age of the one whose death is announced — are still vigorously maintained, and are certainly very beautiful. The historic preëminence and present activity of the Moravian Church in missionary enterprise is too well known to need more than mere mention. Compared with the competing and disputatious sects of the Middle West, the Unitas Fratrum — as the Moravian body is strictly called — as I saw it in eastern Pennsylvania, seemed to have a peculiarly untroubled and untroubling faith.

Bethlehem, as I approached it in the train that ran along the picturesque Lehigh River, reminded me somewhat of Durham, in England — only there was not the squalor that disfigures so many cities of the older country, and there was no Cathedral on the heights. Of all the places I have seen in the United States, only Charleston, South Carolina, and New Orleans approach it in quaintness. The old Moravian hostelry, the old burying-ground with gravestones lying flat on the ground and placed in strict order according to the dates of death without regard to family groups, the low stone buildings — everything in the old portion of the town seemed part of a fit setting for the religious customs, the musical atmosphere, the historic liturgy, and the traits of sturdiness, simplicity, and self-forgetfulness in the character of its people. I remember one lane in particular, flanked by high brown walls, over which hung the limbs of fruit-trees in full blossom. Not half the old-world charm of the town has ever been described. On the other hand, the people have been so frequently caricatured by over-enthusiastic reporters that they have come to be thought of as peculiarly different in manners and dress from other folk. An editor on whom I called showed very plainly that he was tired of being "written up." Ministers were at first unresponsive to my inquiries. A vivacious and charming member of the Moravian Church, the wife of a mechanical engineer of the iron-works, told me a story illustrative of the wide-spread popular fallacy as to the queerness of the Moravian people. She was one of a number of young people, all Moravians, who were among the guests at a dance in Philadelphia. During the evening she was introduced to a lady of evident intelligence, who, after some conversation, exclaimed:

"Oh, have you seen them?"

"Seen whom?"

" Why, the Moravians. They say a party of them are to be here to-night. I'm just dying to see them. Why, you know, it will be just the strangest thing! They wear a peculiar costume and all that. I wish they would come. I don't see what makes them so late."

She was talking to a Moravian and did not know it.

In one respect the Moravians are a peculiar people. Their church music is a heritage they jealously and enthusiastically prize. Nowhere else in America has the St. Matthew " Passion " of Bach been sung, as it was intended to be, not for a concert performance but for a church service, with the chorales taken up by a congregation of people who had been familiar with them from childhood. It was in Bethlehem that both the Christmas Oratorio and the so-called B minor Mass of Bach had their first complete American rendition. During my visit rehearsals for a three-day Bach music festival to be given by a chorus from the community were in progress. I have heard technically better singing of Bach, but none so convincingly genuine. The sight of the children who were in the chorus, and the sound of their voices, were alone almost enough to make one a convert to the faith.

The account of the ceremonies of the church and of the preaching of the ministers was interesting. So were the statements which two ministers made independently concerning the social conditions among the workingmen in the ironworks, the rebuffs which the Church had met with from the representatives of the owners, the effect of the breaking up of family life by modern conditions of labor, the consequences following the influx of foreigners, and the relation of the university to the community. But the one impression which I carried away from Bethlehem was of a community whose character had been created and was still molded by a religious faith which was retaining much of its pristine power through the use of traditional, but vitalizing, forms of great beauty.

COLORADO

XIII

COLORADO

THE three parts into which places innumerable have been divided since Julius Cæsar wrote his Commentaries have their counterparts in Colorado: the City, the Resort, and the Camp. It is true there is a fourth part, the Ranch, which in certain respects is more important than all the others, for the agricultural products of the State form a larger part of its wealth than its minerals. In comparison to the Ranch, therefore, the City is a dependent, the Resort is a parasite, and the Camp is a poor relation. For our purposes, however, we will assume that all Colorado is divided into three parts.

Those who go from the East to Colorado — whether it is to the City, or to the Resort, or to the Camp — are put to a thorough and very

wholesome test as regards both character and
religious faith.   This test consists in being
granted a very great freedom from the conventional standards of morality and religion.
A case somewhat parallel is that of the native
of southern Italy who emigrates to America.
In the country of his birth he is expected by
everybody to conform to the observances of
the Church.   In his adopted country he finds
many who conform to the observances of other
churches, and some who conform to none at all.
For the first time he has the choice between
religion and no religion.   If he is a genuinely
devout Roman Catholic, he will continue to
attend mass and perform his religious obligations.   If he is a mere formalist, and happens
not to take up his residence in a community
practically transplanted bodily from his native
soil, or to come under the influence of an especially active priest, he will fall away from the
practices which at home were a matter of
course, and be content with having recourse to
the Church only as a matter of expediency —
and habit — in greatest extremities.   The result
is that among Italians in America it is perhaps
more common to find, on the one hand, open
hostility to the Church than in Italy, and, on

the other hand, more vital and active life within
the Church itself.   A closer parallel is that of
the boy who goes from his village home to the
city. The fact that in the village he is known
to almost everybody binds him to do what his
family and his acquaintances do.   The fact, on
the other hand, that in the city no one he knows
will notice his absence from church or his
presence in the dive leaves him free to choose,
and he will choose the one or the other according to the inward force of will rather than the
outward force of opinion.   The result is that
among young men in the city are found both
wilder dissipation and sturdier self-control than
among the young men of a village community.
In much the same way, the man from the East
who goes to the City, the Resort, or the Camp
of Colorado finds himself confronted with the
necessity of making his own choice in matters
of conduct and faith.   This is not so much
because he is presented with new alternatives, as
is true in the case of the immigrant; nor so
much because he is no longer subject to the
regard of interested neighbors, as is true in the
case of the village boy in the city — though both
these facts are contributing causes — as because
he has entered into a life essentially uncon-

ventional. In the East a man gets material advantage by leading an outwardly respectable life, and even by being identified, either in person or through his family, to some extent at least, with the Church. In Colorado an outwardly respectable life, it is safe to say, is not any disadvantage to a man, but it is hardly safe to say that in the Camp, in the Resort, or even in the City it brings any immediate visible reward; and as for church membership, perhaps the safest thing to say is that there is less excuse for moral anomalies among church members than in most places in America. The result is that, according not only to what I heard of, but also to what I saw, in Colorado as in no other region I visited, open, unshamed violation of common morality exists side by side with genuine, courageous, and single-minded religious faith and life.

It was only a brief glimpse that I had of the City. That was enough, however, to include the extremes characteristic of the State. Denver is a city of many fine streets and some forlorn quarters; of dives and of churches; of *nouveaux riches* and of cultivated men. At the time I was there, it happened that, on the one hand, I heard a considerable discussion — made possible by woman suffrage — concerning the effect upon municipal conditions of the votes cast by inmates of disorderly houses; and, on the other hand, I attended a reception at which there were present the presidents of four important colleges. No city, however, can wholly withstand the encroachments of conventionalism. So Denver is growing more conventional — in matters of institutional religion at any rate. Most of its churches, like most of the churches in the cities of the East and the Middle West, have been moving uptown, following along in the procession of the respectable. Some of these churches are very prosperous. One in particular that I saw, owing in part to the natural growth of this Western city, owing in part to the efficiency of its pastor, seemed like one of those Western corn-fields in which the corn grows so fast that you can hear it crackle as it grows. But this church was composed mainly of what an Englishman would call middle-class people, and what most Americans think of when they visualize the great Sovereign Citizen.

In spite of this tendency to conventionality, one man I met has remained during these years an apostle of the unconventional. This was

"Parson Tom," as he is universally known, the minister of a Congregational church. He was a member of the City Council. In order to find him I had to go to the City Hall. As we came down the steps together, a man and a woman, both poorly dressed, stopped him and held a hurried, brief consultation with him. The parson-councilman explained that this man and wife had come to him for a chance to get a job under the city government. Here was one minister who believed there was no reason why a minister should not use for unselfish ends a means of "reaching" people which the ward boss uses too often for corrupt and selfish ends. We walked along the street to his new church building, then in process of construction. A drunken man hailed him in response to a touch on the shoulder. Two little children greeted him as an old friend. A man, evidently a day-laborer, asked for a chance to see him. So the appearance of the parson's stalwart figure evoked from one after another expressions of friendliness and confidence. And all this was on the edge of the "scarlet district." He told me stories of the turmoil in the city occasioned by the influx of men who left Chicago during the panic of '93; how troops came by train to the fort, how the banks were used as arsenals, how with others he had succeeded in preventing starvation by supplying the men with bologna sausages, how he had had to address the crowds, how with others he succeeded in sending the men out with State money to the Missouri River, how afterwards in Memphis he came across a man who said to him, "I'm one of those you sent out; there are five hundred of us here working on the levee, and we'll give you an ovation"; and how he had met others of those men in all sorts of places between Chicago and San Francisco. The minister who has had influence with laboring men, individually and in large bodies, under both ordinary and extraordinary circumstances, is rare. The views of such a man on the religious life of workingmen are, I think, worth summarizing. In the first place, he was convinced that it was one thing to win the approval of the labor agitator and quite another to win the approval of the great body of wage-earners. In the second place, he recognized certain obstacles in the very unconventionality of Western life: the unreligious atmosphere which, though uncongenial to cant and pretense, is also uncongenial to devoutness; the open Sunday, with its "splendid opportunities for staying away from church"; the many organizations which are more attractive to men under ordinary conditions than the churches are, though wanting in the message which the Church has for great exigencies; and the tendency of the Church to revert to traditional methods even under such new conditions as those of a Colorado city.

We soon came to the new church building. It was only a block or two from the old building. He explained his action in remaining on the edge of the "scarlet district" by saying, "If you set a trap on the hill to catch a fish in the river, you'll be a long time catching him. I've got about two-thirds of the city to look after." Yet his work was very far from being merely what is termed "rescue work." His chief interest was in the poor of the district, who were forced by circumstances to live in an environment full of vice and shame. He felt keenly the unfairness to these poor of permitting disorderly houses to exist among them. He has shown the courage of his convictions by refusing to leave this district. His mother, he told me, sharing his convictions, shares also in his work, for, though she is seventy-five years old, she drives about with a little Shetland pony, distributing to the needy. And now that he had to build a new church, he chose a site where it would primarily serve the neighborhood, and only secondarily be accessible to those of his congregation whose lines are fallen in pleasanter places.

In the Resort, many of the people are, of course, enforced idlers. Since they are there either because of their own ill health or because of the ill health of some member of the family, such people, with more time than they know how to occupy wisely, and more money than they know how to spend judiciously, are strongly tempted to welcome their release from conventionality by releasing themselves also from common moral obligation. Those people, therefore, whose conduct in the East is bound chiefly by a sense of propriety, make the discovery, soon after their arrival in Colorado, that their conduct there is under scarcely any bonds whatever. Those, on the other hand, who carry their moral principles with them find those principles as unaffected by the lessening of the pressure of conventionalism as by the lessening of the pressure of the atmosphere. Take away the sanction of convention, and the goats of their own free will separate themselves from the sheep. A sojourn in Colorado Springs has afforded many men and women, who have abundant time and money, a very close approximation to the modern theologian's conception of the Day of Judgment. Only, conventionalism does not wholly disappear; so the approximation is but earthly, after all. It naturally follows from all this that such people as make a pretense of religion in the East continue in that pretense when they reach the Colorado Resort — so far as they continue in it at all — less as a studied means for self-advancement than as a habit of which they are more or less unconscious.

Such a condition cannot fail to strike one who cares at all for reality in religion as being constitutionally wholesome. In the first place, it prevents the sanctimonious hypocrite from deceiving almost every well-informed person, except possibly himself. No circumstance can ever wholly cure self-deception. In the second place, it makes possible a genuineness in religious life which is at best limited under any other condition.

That such a condition of genuineness in conduct, in spite of its concomitant open immorality, can do away with much of the misun-

derstanding between organized wage-earners
and organized Christian people was illustrated
by what a carpenter, himself a man not only of
deep religious convictions but also of fine fiber
and native refinement, told me. He prefaced
his tale, which others corroborated and partly
amplified, by saying that industrial conditions
in Colorado Springs had been for years exceptionally easy. There had been such a continu-
ous demand for labor in the building trades
that the wages of carpenters, for instance, had
risen in nine years from $2.75 a day to $3.50,
and the hours of labor per day had decreased
from ten to eight. This process, moreover, had
gone on without a strike and with only one instance of temporary suspension of work, and
that had occurred by a misunderstanding of
the state of affairs on the part of outsiders.
Under these conditions the relations between
employers and employed had come to be pleasant. The men did as much work in eight
hours as they had been accustomed to do in
ten, for, as it was explained, "they feel that
the conditions are happy, and want to make an
equivalent." In reply to my inquiries as to
how these pleasant relations between labor and
capital were brought about, I heard from more

than one source the following story, in about
the form which I give it:

Several years ago, when the wage-earner who
was mainly responsible for the undertakings I
am about to describe first entered "the organization," he was convinced that the mutual feeling between labor and capital could be made
more cordial. At that time certain strikes in
the West had made this feeling especially bitter.
At Colorado Springs some union men, of rather
fiery temper and of disposition violently opposed
to religion, attempted, in spite of the easy
industrial conditions there, to intensify these
bitter feelings. The member of whom I have
spoken, being chairman, could not take the
floor to counsel a better spirit, so he suggested
that the union institute a series of talks on labor
problems, make the meetings open, and send
special invitations to ministers and to employers
of labor. The first speaker was selected with
great care; the meetings were held; a number
of ministers became interested, and their verdict
was, "Why, this is Christian; it is neither
Anarchy nor Socialism." Then followed labor
conferences. The attendance of the general
public grew so that it was necessary to hire the
high-school building for the meetings. The

subjects, instead of being general, were selected with regard to municipal matters of current interest. The question of municipal ownership of street railways grew out of the refusal of the local street railway company to hold to its promise of granting free transfers, because it was too expensive. As this materially affected the wage-earners, they took up at the conference the cost of running street-cars. Investigation showed that the company was using money to boom suburban lots. As Colorado Springs owned the water plant, a good contrast was afforded between private and public ownership of municipal monopoly. In a similar way the ownership of the electric light plant was discussed. The country was scoured for information. The result was that the rich men of the place and the wage-earners met on the common level of economic facts. The personal meeting brought about a mutual respect for intellectual qualities. The members of the unions and the employers caught the spirit of the undertaking. They learned to speak easily on their feet. Men who had formerly been bitterly opposed to organized labor became friends, because of the reasonableness of the unions. Of course there was no lack of opposition and indifference; of course there were some sad experiences. Certain of the churches and the ministers failed to fall into line. On the other side two of the labor organizations proved unruly. One of these started a movement for higher wages, but failed because it did not get the support of the other unions and the sympathy of the public. The movement resulted, not only in a failure to gain its end, but also in a distinct loss. This was one direct result of the conferences; it gave a new value and sanction to public opinion. Another result was that the support of the conferences by certain churches and ministers heartened that minority in the unions who were genuinely religious, and, as was shown by subsequent events, gave to those who had not been in sympathy with the Church a new conception of institutional religion.

Such was the situation when the Young Men's Christian Association proposed the building of new quarters. Until then the Association had done very little to bring wage-earners into its membership. After these conferences proved successful, the member of the union who had suggested and directed them was chosen, in spite of his modest protest that he was incompetent, as a member of the Board of Directors of the Association. I give his story about the building as nearly as possible in his own words:

"They were talking about getting money for the building. But, as I became acquainted with the new secretary, who had been a wage-earner and was a member of a labor union, 'Here,' said I to him, 'I've got something for you. I want you to go to the organizations.' And I had this advantage, for I could say, 'Boys, here's a man who carries his card.' The responses were generous. I was strengthened, you see, by having a man who was a wage-earner with me. I said, 'When this building is finished we want a label on top.' I spoke to the teamsters, and we got a contribution from them of forty days' work, valued at four dollars a day. They gave it especially on account of their boys. One man — a Bob Ingersoll man — objected, but finally he gave one day's work with three teams — that means twelve dollars. Then the pick and shovel men each promised to give from one to three days' work. In the carpenters' organization the decision was to give one day's work each — in cash, fifteen hundred dollars! So it went. This Young Men's Christian Association building is to be built as the cathedrals of France were

built, by the voluntary and coöperative contribution of the labor of the people. When the
day came, the organizations left their work to
see the breaking of ground. The men wore
ribbons, yellow, pinned on labels, and they were
proud of them. They got out the band. They
had a parade three-quarters of a mile long.
There were the police, the band, the high-school
cadets, and the labor organizations with their
banners, and each man carried a flag. This
will show the interest: An old German, who is
a Grand Army man, and who says that there is
only one holiday, Decoration Day, because he
was 'in it,' had never lost a half-day's work
otherwise; but, don't you know, he gave half
a day for this parade! Another man gave a
dollar and said: 'This is all I can afford, but
I want you to take this dollar and buy some
bricks, and mark them, and put them in the
front where I can see them.' The teamster
who was to haul out the first load was chosen
by his organization; others were grouped about.
That's the way the ground was broken for the
building. While this good feeling exists we
want all to have a part in the better things this
building stands for." "Yes," he added, in
answer to a remark of mine, " it seems that

I've had a part in this, for which I am very grateful."

This is what a recreation and health resort has contributed toward the solution of one of the most vexing problems in the religious life of America.[1] It is unquestionable, however, that the method would have been ineffectual if it had not been for certain individual men — chiefly three: the member of the union who suggested the project, the President of Colorado College, and the Secretary of the Association. As in every other successful effort for practical religious life that I have seen, the chief agency in this was forceful personality.

The way to the Camp lay over the snow-streaked mountains. The train crawled up the grade. Soon Colorado Springs lay like a map on the table-land below. Up went the train, along gorges, around almost spiral curves. Suddenly it stopped with a jerk. The road was new, and the melting snow had brought down a mass of loosened earth and rock upon the tracks. Stock-brokers, miners, bankers, tourists, left the train and walked

[1] The Young Men's Christian Associations of Cleveland and Dayton, Ohio, have succeeded in enlisting the coöperation of wage-earners, though in quite different fashion from that I have just described. I was not fortunate enough to include in my observations either of these Ohio cities.

ahead. There men with crowbars, picks, and
shovels were clearing away the *débris*. Soon
darkness fell. In the dim light of lanterns the
huge rocks glistened like snow. The gorges
grew black and seemingly bottomless. The
screech of a whistle echoed and reëchoed. A
gleam of light shone on the rocks and was
reflected in sinuous golden curves on the edge
of the rails. The passengers who had gone
beyond the landslide scattered to points of
safety as the train from Cripple Creek flashed
and rumbled past. Immediately an exchange
of passengers was made. The two huge loco-
motives glared and snorted at each other.
Over the pile of stones and earth between
them, human creatures, like midgets beneath
the masses of rock, darted in and out of the
shadows. A man carrying a rifle guarded
the express matter. The steam from the en-
gines formed a vast sheet on which the moving
shadows of gigantic men passed. Prismatic
blues and yellows edged this sheet of vapor
with color. Yet this scene of light was but
a spot in the enveloping blackness. Deep
down I knew, I felt, but could not see, was the
precipitous slope of the mountain-side. Then

slowly the train started. Within the car the conversation was of mines and stocks. Another sudden stop. Another landslide ahead. After a long delay the obstruction was removed with dynamite. Then hours of cautious creeping in the darkness. Suddenly in the velvety blackness below gleamed a mass of constellations, as if these heights were indeed the very border of the earth, and we were gazing down at the sky beneath us. These nether stars were the lights of Cripple Creek.

It was after two o'clock Sunday morning when we reached the station. From a street near by, brilliantly lighted, where men and women could be seen entering and leaving the dives and resorts of vice, came the sound of dance music and revelry. At the big hotel gambling-wheels and slot-machines were in evidence. Yet it was in this city, which is called the Camp, that I found, when at last daylight returned, a church with as vigorous and genuine a religious spirit as it has ever been my good fortune to see. Here, in the midst of a district which comprised a population of fifty thousand, where ten years before there had been nothing but grazing-ground

for cattle, there was evident a stalwart faith
that is rarely developed in communities outwardly more civilized.

The small Congregational church was filled
with a congregation made up largely of men.
There was a quality of spontaneity in the service that is not too common in public worship.
The sermon was rugged in diction, thoughtful,
and genuine — every word of it. The Bible
class after the morning service was marked by
an interchange of ideas, real ideas. It seemed
incredible even at the time, but it was invigorating. I had occasion afterwards to feel the
grip of some of those miners' hands. That
was invigorating, too.

The minister explained, as he pointed out the
foundations of a new building in front of his
church, that there were the beginnings of a
parish house, some day to contain a gymnasium,
swimming-tank, reading-room, and other means
of wholesome recreation. It was designed to
afford young men some other place besides
"Hell's Acre" to which they might go for
amusement. Where was the money to come
from for the cost of construction? The minister did not know. Nobody in Cripple Creek
seems to know just where money is coming

from. One thing was clear: this parish house was not a "drawing card." As the minister stated it, in order to get hold of men in Cripple Creek, it does no good to shake the tree; you must pick them by hand.

This method of building the house is characteristic of the Camp. It is the abode of idealists. "There are three stages in the history of a mining camp," said the minister. "The first is the stage of the wilderness, without habitation. The second follows the discovery of gold, when the miners, too busy in the early work of prospecting to think of comfort, live in shacks. This invariably ends with a destructive fire. Then comes the stage of permanent building. It is when the miner is living in his shack that he is most luxurious, for then he is really — in his imagination — not living in his shack at all, but in marble and in down." A church in a mining camp cannot wholly escape this idealism. This is one result of the unconventionality of Cripple Creek.

But the men of the Camp do not stop with ideals. They are men who do things. And the church is of the same sort. A church of one hundred members that raises eight hundred dollars in one year for missions is certainly not engaged merely in dreaming.[1] The active energy of the churches in Cripple Creek is, however, to be seen chiefly in the unorganized activity of their individual members. In this respect the Church in the Camp is too much like the Church in the rest of the world.

It is true that even the Camp, unconventional as it is, has not been exempt from doctrinal controversy. I had the privilege of hearing the end of a debate which centered about the meaning in the New Testament of the Greek verb translated " baptize." The minister who began it undertook to prove that it really signified "immerse," and sneeringly challenged a reply. It is hardly necessary to say that the frequenters of "Hell's Acre" registered no protest against either interpretation. In fairness, however, it should be said that this exhibition of denominational pertness was probably unusual, and, at any rate, while it lasted was marked by a vigor and candor wholly appropriate to the character of the region.

Above all, religion in the Camp is saved

[1] A few months after the date of my visit the public gambling-houses were closed and the professional gamblers driven from town. This was due to the energy and courage of a few men in the churches backed up by public opinion and the integrity of a judge.

from the depredations of its most treacherous enemy — sanctimony. The sanctimonious man is to be found there, I know, for I saw him, but he is " sized up." If he is a vicious hypocrite, he has no chance, for, as one man expressed it, " vice is so open here that a hypocrite can't live a loose life on the quiet "; consequently he takes, or appears to take, " a tremendous tumble." If he is merely a Pharisee, he fares no better, for a Pharisee is only a religious or moral snob, and in a mining camp there are too many grim and exciting realities for men to stand in awe of any kind of snobbery. The practical absence of all moral and religious pretense enhances the power of a life governed by genuine moral principle and religious impulse. Good coin is more efficient as a circulating medium when practicable counterfeits are made impossible.

Certain practical results from this absence of pretense were evident to me in Cripple Creek. In the first place, since most opposition to religion is really a form of resentment against imposture, open confession of religion in Cripple Creek, just because it was almost certain to be genuine, appeared to meet with no ridicule or antagonism. When, for instance, on Sunday night the minister and I entered a disreputable dance-hall, our presence was unnoticed although my companion wore a clerical costume. A few doors away a " Gospel Mission," with dives on each side, was being conducted without the least sign of molestation; and near by in the same street, where the sidewalks were used with almost the same freedom that the houses were, the Salvation Army was carrying on a meeting, and was not only unmolested, so I was assured, but also thoroughly respected. Such, I understood, had been the experience of the Salvation Army continually at Cripple Creek. Indeed, the men of the Camp, because they live in an atmosphere of hatred of cant, are emphatically open-minded, and will give a hearing to a preacher as scarcely any other body of men will do. My clerical Congregational guide said that he often had preached to crowds on the streets, and had always been respectfully heard; that, in fact, some of the most active members of his church he first saw in a street crowd at a preaching. This, then, I noticed, was one result of the absence of cant — that the religious life was accorded respect.

In the second place, certain methods of religious work that elsewhere would have the taint of conventionalism and would seem pietistic seemed in the mining camp to be spontaneous and genuine. Neither in the accounts I heard of "conversions" nor in personal experiences in the church did I discover anything either unctuous or perfunctory. A spirit of genuineness invests even conventional forms with new value.

In the third place, the freedom from pretense increased the value of the test, "By their fruits ye shall know them." The mine superintendent who succeeded in bringing about the regular closing of his mine every Sunday testified by his action to the strength of his religious convictions all the more because he curried no man's favor by his action. To what a different tree the same fruit may sometimes bear witness was illustrated by another mine superintendent who closed his mine on Sundays while his wife visited him from the East. That bit of pretense was not indigenous to the soil of the Camp. When left to itself, Cripple Creek may be immoral, but it certainly is temperamentally sincere. For that reason I could more readily believe the testimony of the superintendent of a mine that he wanted religious men to work in his mine, because they were free from vicious habits, they were more efficient workmen, and took more interest in the company's welfare and success than others did. Cripple Creek, just because it is free from pretense, places upon the religious life a very real and entirely distinctive ethical value.

The City, the Resort, and the Camp, each in its own way, set before men with unconcealed contrast the good and the evil from which to choose. There is little mingling of the black with the white. Somehow it is very wholesome — this facing of the fact of evil, and making deliberate choice for or against it. Whether you think or not, as I do, that it is exhilarating, it is certainly true that in Colorado, as in few other regions, the Church has a freedom to make clear that there is no compromise between the evil that men should hate and shun and the good that men should choose, the Christ they should follow, the God they should love and serve.

SATIS SUPERQUE

XIV

SATIS SUPERQUE

THIS book really ends with the preceding chapter. Whatever is hereinafter written is almost entirely outside of the original plan, which was merely to record observations, not to make wide generalizations. It was inevitable, however, that, as a result of my journey, I should reach some general conclusions as to religious life in America, as readers of the preceding chapters have undoubtedly already discovered. Inasmuch as several readers of the articles in periodical form have expressed a desire to know what these conclusions are, it is not unlikely that others may have a similar desire. For that reason I incorporate into this chapter certain questions in much the same form in which they were put to me, and to each one attach an answer.

To what is the manifest reaction against religious life and observance in New England due? — to a laxity in theology, or to an intellectual revolt against the doctrines of Puritanism? This question assumes as true the decadence of religion in rural New England, of which much has recently been said and written. That decadence has been sometimes over-emphasized. The picture of it has too often been copied from the representations of the Yankee who has fallen into the habit of contrasting with " the good old times " all the evils of the present, who is experiencing "the sadness of survival," and makes the most of it. Nevertheless, after all is said, some decadence is very real. It has unquestionably been accompanied by a looseness of thinking, a flabbiness of mind, that is evident not only in theology, but in all intellectual processes. I am inclined to think that this mental softness is a result rather than a cause; that it is in part a consequence of the loss of distinctness in ideas that is suffered whenever men replace narrow conceptions with broader ones; and, in part, a consequence of economic change. Much of the disregard of religious observance is due less to a deliberate intellectual revolt than to a natural reaction against the harsh doctrines and more particularly the practical severities of previous generations. I know that many men and women, whose childhood was made miserable by the heartless and unlovely form assumed by the piety of their parents, have, in their attempt to avoid making their children miserable, neglected to give them even elementary religious and moral instruction. The uneducated Yankee infidel is the project of an unintelligent reaction from an unreligious pietism. Apathy, however, is more serious than open revolt, and the disregard of religion in New England is in its nature not so much antagonistic as apathetic. The cause for this, I believe, is not reaction against Puritanism, nor laxity in theology, but a social condition. New England has been gradually but steadily bled. Its most vital element, the enterprising young people, has for years been drawn into other parts of the Nation. Religious indifference, as well as intellectual inertness, in New England is only one part of the general languor that is a symptom of anæmia.

Is there likely to be, under present theological conditions, a revival of genuine religious belief and conduct in New England? If there is to be such renewal of life, two conditions must be fulfilled. First, the process of draining off the best elements of the population must be diminished; second, there must be an intelligent and deliberate effort, impelled by enthusiasm, to adjust the work of the churches to the changed social environment and intellectual temper. In diminishing emigration theological ideas can of course have no effect. One rural district in Maine, for instance, which thirty years ago maintained a school of forty pupils, now sends to its little tumble-down school-house only four children. The lifelessness of that school-room can scarcely be imagined. One day, when I chanced to visit it, the mosquitoes were swarming in by the loosely flapping netting at the windows because the teacher and her pupils lacked brains or energy enough to tack the netting down in place. Two of the children were almost as untrained as the creatures of the woods. In another country school which I entered during recess the boys were stupidly gathered about the window. They had not life enough even for play. They responded willingly enough when I proposed to teach them the game of "duck on the rock," but inertly ceased all play as soon as I left them. Such communities as those, where even the boys lack zest for outdoor play, do not need doctrine, harsh or mellow, but an infusion of new life. I think I am not alone in the opinion that already present economic conditions are permitting New England to recover its vitality. Moreover, there are signs that the churches are trying to adapt themselves to the changed environment and intellectual temper. Not a few of the younger ministers, who recognize that religion cannot without disaster be severed from the multiform activities of humanity, are using their wits as well as losing their own lives in introducing new elements of vitality into communities that have contributed their native elements of vitality to the large cities and the great West. In one respect, of course, religious belief — as distinguished from ecclesiastical dogma — is at the source of this effort for adjustment; for when ministers believe, as they do far more strongly than they did a generation or two ago, that God is in all his world, that his kingdom is not a mere demesne around the pulpit and the "family altar," but an all-inclusive empire, they will not be satisfied with letting economic and social reinvigoration come as the selfishness of men may dictate without the contributing force of religious impulse. What sacrifice such belief may involve is indicated by the experience of a certain young minister who went directly from the theological seminary into a lumber town of New Hampshire. There, under the auspices of the missionary society of his denomination, he organized a church. Highly educated, he devoted his mental acquirements to the improvement of the town schools. Athletic, he used his physique in compelling the disorderly element in the population to respect if not wholly to obey the laws. Bred in the lumber regions, he helped to cut the wood for the church building he succeeded in erecting. Broad in his sympathies and interests, he included in his church building a reading-room and gymnasium. Distrustful of traditionalism, he did not hesitate to make his preaching and teaching accord with modern knowledge. Strongly evangelical in temperament, he drew people into the church by the earnestness with which he declared his faith in the power of his crucified and risen Master, Christ. At the end of a few years — perhaps some half-dozen — he had transformed that community. But he had given his life. From sheer exhaustion he died, broken down in health and mind, a vicarious sacrifice for the people he had served. Though I know of no other such man as this, yet I do know that, in different ways, in accordance with different temperaments and different communities, other men are denying them- selves much which, being human, they prize — comfort, advancement, congenial friends, ap- preciation, even opportunities for their own mental and moral growth — in order that they may put what vitality they have into lethargic communities. In brief, then, I look for a steady renewal of religious life in New Eng- land, first, because I think the economic pro- cess which has resulted in its present lethargy has spent its force and in some places is being reversed; second, because many of the younger generation of ministers, governed by the belief that nothing human is outside of the sphere of religion, are giving, with no small cost to themselves, which is the more praiseworthy as well as the more effectual because largely un- premeditated, the benefit of their intelligent energy to supply the very diverse needs of their communities.

As the South develops, is it likely to go through the same transition as that which is

observable in New England? Without attempting to dogmatize, I think I can say pretty
confidently that it is not. For at least these
three reasons: In the first place, the economic
and social changes that have been taking place
in the South during the past generation have
been very different — in some respects quite
opposite — to those which have been taking
place in New England. I do not need to point
out the contrast in detail; it is entirely too
well known. The effect of economic change
upon a Southern rural community I have
already had occasion to point out in the chapter on "A Virginia Country Rector." It is
sufficient here to say that whereas the typical
New Englander of to-day is reminiscently de-
spondent, his typical Southern contemporary is
hopeful; the former has felt the loss of social
vitality, the latter is just beginning to feel its
influx. With this difference between the economic conditions of New England and those
of the South, their religious conditions cannot
be the same. In the second place, the orthodoxy of the South, though it is quite as traditional and in form is quite as stern as that of
New England ever was, is by no means marked
by the actual practical austerities that made the

Calvinism of Puritan New England at last unendurable. Though there are in the South many of the same mind with the Presbyterian minister who in conversation with me protested against the belief in the universal Fatherhood of God and the brotherhood of all men as a virtual denial of the Christian faith, they belie their harsh theories by the habitual suavity of their manner and kindliness of their heart. There can hardly be the same reaction against Southern orthodoxy as there has been against the Puritanical rigor of the North. In the third place, as is indicated in the chapter on " New Religious Tendencies in the Old South," theological ideas at variance with traditional religious theories are being diffused very gradually and quietly through the South, almost without observation. They made their way in very different fashion in New England — creating turbulence, dissension, enmities, and schisms. The difference is that between a conquering army of invaders and a vast number of quietly straggling immigrants. The modern conceptions that descended upon New England as young and immature soldiers with the roar of cannon have in the course of years become good citizens, and are now going South as responsible middle-aged homesteaders. There they are meeting with suspicion, but not with armed resistance. The South is undoubtedly undergoing a transition from old to new religious ideas, but the process is likely to be not revolutionary but gradual, peaceful, and possibly therefore the more thorough.

Is the religious condition of the negro improving or deteriorating? Concerning the negro race as a whole I have already expressed the judgment that no safe generalization can be made. This, however, can be said with certainty, that the race is showing both the good and the ill effects of liberty. Large numbers are wholly unfit for conditions of freedom, and are rapidly succumbing to their environment. Such show their deterioration physically, morally, and religiously, by their susceptibility to disease, their non-resistance to evil, and their lapse from even the hysterical forms of religious emotionalism. On the other hand, large numbers — larger than is generally known even in the South — have found in the conditions of freedom their chance for physical, moral, and religious development. Among such the development possibly has been too rapid, too much of the nature of sudden reaction, to be alto-

gether wholesome.   One negro minister said —
and I had good reason to value his judgment in
this respect — that his congregation, through
fear of emotional excesses, to which, as a people,
they felt themselves to be peculiarly liable, had
acquired the fault of unresponsiveness and
frigidity. If a race is to be judged by its
leaders, the religious condition of the negro in
the South has much in it of promise.

Signs are not lacking of the political supremacy of the West; what is its religious influence?   There are two distinct regions in what
is commonly called the West; between the Middle West and the pioneer country there is the
strongest kind of contrast.   Neither of them, it
seems to me, is influential in forming theological conceptions; both of them are influential in
suggesting experiments in church methods.   In
these respects they are alike, but, as far as I
could see, in no other.   Before going to the
Middle West I was led into expecting to find it
governed by traditionalism.   In that I was mistaken.   The Middle West is no more enterprising in business affairs than it is in religious
schemes.   Indeed, nowhere else has Christianity
been so diversely garbed or so variously vul-
garized.   At the same time, religion in the

Middle West is essentially conventional. Its standards are, generally speaking, external rather than intrinsic. This, however, is only a part — an unfortunately necessary part — of the process by which a composite population is making itself homogeneous. The social consciousness which is a result of that process has fitted the Middle West for performing what is and will increasingly continue to be its chief service to the religious life of the Nation — namely, its constant insistence, partly by word, more effectively by example, upon the social bearing of religion. The pioneer West, in distinction from the middle region, may be godless, wicked, sordid — though I do not say that it is — but above all things it is genuine. It is probably too new and too isolated to have much influence upon the country at large, but what influence it exerts in religion must be in creating and intensifying the hatred of sham and the love of reality and candor.

How much of an ethical force are the churches of this country? Not by any means so great as they ought rightfully to be. This is partly because they spend so much time in trying to satisfy the insatiable human craving for superficial speculative philosophy by retailing old dogmas supposed to be true because they are old, or by manufacturing new creeds supposed to be true because they are new. It is partly also because they too frequently lack the courage to deal plainly with specific evils, for fear of unpleasant consequences. Such courage is not always shown as it was by those ministers in a Southern city I passed through, who, during the season when the races were exclusively engrossing the attention of even members of their churches, preached very directly and pointedly against the then prevalent madness of gambling. In spite, however, of their defects, the churches are a tremendously strong ethical force in the life of the people; though I know superlatives are dangerous, I do not hesitate to say, the strongest. Indeed, the churches cannot help exerting a very distinct ethical influence, if only for the fact that they are constantly engaged in making known the greatest body of ethical teaching in the world — the Bible. Even men who are non-church-goers are frankly shocked when a church falls away from high ethical standards. Nothing can more definitely indicate the extent of the Church's ethical influence. The fact is that the Church is universally subjected to a

critical estimate according to ideals by which
no other institution is measured. In comparison with such ideals the Church is obviously
defective as an ethical force; in comparison
with other institutions the Church is immeasur-
ably superior. This I found to be manifestly
true in all regions.

Are the churches intellectually adjusted to
the life of to-day? There is no weakness of
the Church which I found more obvious than
its failure to adjust itself to intellectual standards that obtain in all life outside the Church.
This weakness is so wide in its extent that the
church which is intellectually modern is usually
self-complacent — not to say intellectually
snobbish — because of its strength in this one
respect. In general, ministers, as I met them,
are very much better acquainted with contemporary scientific and philosophic thought, and
very much more in agreement with it, than laymen. This, of course, is not to be deplored;
but it did seem to me deplorable that so many
ministers among those with whom I talked felt
themselves subject to a humiliating supervision,
and not infrequently constraint, exercised by
laymen whose mental attitude had been unaffected by modern knowledge, except to be
made more obstinately traditional.

Is the Church developing or losing sympathy with the working classes? The cases I saw of conscious attempts to fashion the Church into shape to suit the demands of wage-earners were sporadic. Their number, I think, is increasing. Such attempts are indicative of a growing desire on the part of the Church to obliterate in religious life the class distinctions that have grown up in consequence of present industrial conditions. I think that along with this desire is a growing sympathy with labor organizations as forces which, in spite of their frequent exhibitions of unintelligence, selfishness, and rancor, are means by which the Church may approach and benefit large numbers of men. The real feeling of the Church has often been obscured, as I have once before indicated, by the attitude of superiority affected by men and women prominent in the Church, and on that account naturally but mistakenly supposed to be representative of it.

If the working classes are perceptibly losing their confidence in the Church, what is to be the outcome? Can it be determined by anything that the Church, and sincere believers and workers in the Church, can do to bring the Church back to the people? The outcome of the present relation between the Church and

such working people as are not of the Church
can be determined only by the Church. The
burden of bringing about a change rests upon
the Church, not upon the alienated classes.
That the burden does not justly belong altogether where it actually rests will make no
difference in the degree of its weight. Indeed,
it is one function of the Church to bear unjust
conditions, as its Master did, and by bearing
cure them. Without question the willingness
to accept the entire responsibility of securing
the confidence of those workingmen who are
now indifferent or antagonistic exists in the
Church; but it lacks adequate expression.
The Church needs to direct its power of intolerance — of which it has sufficient — against
those of its own constituency who are misrepresenting it and denying the spirit of its faith
by intensifying class antagonism. One thing
that the sincere believers and workers in the
Church can do to bring back the Church to the
people is to follow in this respect the guidance
of its ministers rather than its "pillars." In
the meantime the sympathy that is too little
expressed is more effective than is ordinarily
known. Here it may be opportune to observe
that, in spite of a frequently expressed opinion

to the contrary, the Church holds popular confidence to a remarkable degree. This can be
especially seen when any great philanthropic
service is to be rendered; the appeal is first of
all to the Church. This is true whether the
project is the building of a village school-house
or the relief of destitution following some great
calamity of national importance.

Is there a tendency toward Christian unity,
not of organization, but of feeling? In other
words, are Christian people pulling together or
pulling apart? The accounts I heard concerning
the sharp practices employed by ministers to
gain advantages over what they counted rival
denominations made belief in a real and earnest
tendency toward Christian unity very difficult.
For instance, one Episcopal rector, of it matters not where, told me how he had been ob-
structed in his plan to enlarge a mission which
his church maintained. He had gone to a
woman, a relative of his, but an adherent of
another denomination, to purchase from her a
lot of land in the vicinity of his mission, for
a new building. Her pastor being informed of
this fact, and knowing that the Episcopal mission was in a critical period because it was
forced to move, privately induced his parish-

ioner to give this land to her own church for a new mission, as a rival to that which had already been long established as the only one in the immediate region. When asked by the rector for an explanation, he showed pride in his strategic move, making as his only defense the gratuitous assumption, "You would have done the same thing if you had been in my place." Another minister, Congregational, told me that to his town, in which his was the only church, came a visiting minister of another denomination, with the purpose of establishing a second church. The Congregational minister, believing that this church should be established if it were needed, gave the visitor not only a welcome but an opportunity to state his case from the pulpit of the Congregational church. After accepting the hospitality and making his appeal, the visitor undertook, before he left the church building, to induce one of the more active of his host's congregation to enter the rival enterprise he was trying to establish. No amount of merely sentimental talk about common aims for the salvation of souls can make much real headway against such violations of strict honesty and ordinary courtesy as these. My experiences, however, lead me to believe that such practices are exceptional, and, when they occur, are reprehended by the public opinion of the churches. Against them the real counteracting force is to be found in movements for the united action of churches and Christian people.

Is there any possibility, however remote, of a working union of the various Protestant sects? I think that such possibility is indicated by the various instances which came under my observation of organic effort: ministers' associations, church federations, and other interdenominational movements, especially those among young people, those for moral reform, and those for missionary enterprise. Nothing that I observed gave any sign of the form which a future working union of Protestant denominations might take. Of only one thing concerning it can I speak with any confidence. Unless present tendencies are reversed, such union will come about through the desire, not for agreement in doctrine, nor for outward parade of power, but for effectiveness in practical religious activity.

Of what value are those institutions of Christianity which are external to the Church? Their value to the Church, as I have already indicated in the answers to the two preceding questions, consists in the fact that they are rudimentary forms of a working union of the different branches of the Church. More than that, they are •doing things which the churches as such have been unable or have simply neglected to do. I found the Young Men's Christian Association notable in both these respects. These modern extra-church institutions, as they may be termed, seem to be doing for the Protestant Church of America what the monastic and mendicant orders did for the Catholic Church of the Middle Ages. The parallel is, of course, far from being exact, but it is close enough to suggest that the Church of to-day will be wise if it will accept and make use of these institutions as the Church of the Middle Ages accepted and made use of the orders.

In regard to commonplace virtues, such as temperance, industry, and the sense of obligation on the part of those who have wealth or education or other advantages, is the present tendency upward or downward? In spite of some experiences which left me in the mood to distrust every appearance of virtue and decency, I found myself at the end of my journey firmly believing that the present ethical tendency is

upward. So far as I could compare my observation with testimony as to past conditions, I
should say that moral standards among Americans to-day are much less formal and provincial
than they were a generation or so ago, much
saner, much more fundamental; based less upon
precept, more upon principle. For instance,
there is probably more drinking but less drunk-
enness; certainly much more respect and regard
for those whose convictions lead them to establish their own temperance by practicing total
abstinence, while there is less vituperation for
those who do not see any necessity for practicing total abstinence in order to establish their
own temperance. Idleness has never, I think,
been a characteristically American fault; I
could not learn that it had increased, though I
did see very plainly that in time spent for recreation there had been a very decided increase
over the time so spent a generation ago. There
seemed to me to be on the part of many individuals a greater sense than ever of responsibility
to society. This is one phase, of course, of the
social consciousness the increase of which was
evident everywhere I traveled.

Is the devotional spirit in religious life increasing or decreasing? Although in general

the tendency in religious life in America seems
to be toward a keener ethical sensitiveness
rather than toward a devouter sentiment, the
effect of my experiences was to increase my
sense of the value and the real permanence of
personal religious feeling. This seems at first
sight to be in face of the fact that there were
signs almost everywhere that the traditional
forms by which such devoutness has been
expressed by Protestants — such as the " prayer-
meeting " and the " experience-meeting " —
are decadent. On the other hand, it is thoroughly in accord with the fact that there were
signs almost everywhere that the use of liturgy
in public worship is becoming more and more
prevalent. What often has been and still is
deplored as a loss of spiritual life is to no
small extent really an improvement in taste.
In other words, it is becoming more and more
recognized that spiritual beauty cannot be cultivated without formal beauty; and, as there is
no trace of formal beauty in the ordinary
prayer-meeting, that some other means of cultivating spiritual beauty must be used. The
substitution of liturgy for the prayer-meeting
is, however, more than a sign of improved taste;
it is a result of changed feelings regarding the

devotional life. Not long ago devout Christians saw no impropriety in talking openly and publicly about their most intimate religious experiences for the edification of other Christians and the conversion of the unregenerate. Now a growing number of Christian people feel that to make a routine matter of public talking about intimate religious experiences not only vulgarizes those experiences, but also fosters self-complacency and invites cant and false pretense. They are consequently reserving their intimate religious experiences for their own private devotions, and for public devotion find satisfaction in those forms which so express common human needs and common human aspirations that a few or many who are gathered together may unite not merely in hearing a clergyman worship for them, but in the very act of worship itself. I have not the space here to show how the historic liturgies also allow for the observance of private devotions at the same time with public worship, so that each may be helped by the other, nor how the abandonment of the prayer-meeting does not mean the abandonment of the best means for cultivating religious experience. I have said enough, however, to show why I believe the decadence of

the devotional spirit because of the desuetude
of the prayer-meeting is more apparent than
real. The chief present impediment to the
growth of the devotional spirit is not the commercial spirit of the day, much less the increased
practical activities of the Church, but the fruitless attempts on the part of both ministers and
laymen to preserve a religious form which,
though of comparatively modern origin as a
regular institution of the Church, is totally
unsuited to the legitimate, not to say wholesome, tendencies of the people. I say wholesome, because I believe that much of the public
expression of personal experience, which the
present tendency is to abandon, is likely to
make the individual self-centered and conspicuous.

Is there more, or is there less, of reverence,
more or less of moral stalwartness, in the
life of American homes? Unquestionably
much in present social conditions is full of
danger to the continuance of wholesome family
life. This danger is quite as apparent in peaceful rural districts as in the big cities. Certainly the religious life of the ordinary American family is not as conspicuous as it once
was. I am inclined to think, on the other

hand, that there has been a markedly increased recognition of the need of early moral and spiritual training of children. The fact is that family life is rather too intimate for the ordinary observer to see much of or to talk much about.

What is the general tendency of views regarding the Bible? People in America may be divided into two categories, determined by their attitude toward the Bible. These may be called, for convenience, the literalists and the idealists. The literalists are those who believe that religious faith should be molded by the Bible; that the Bible is the only true source of Christian belief. This category is not made up wholly of those who are adherents of the Church; indeed, most of the people who are unconnected with any church take this point of view by assuming that no one is a Christian unless he derives his beliefs from the Bible. It is from the literalists — both adherents and non-adherents of the Church — that the new sects derive their supporters. By simply persuading people that the Bible inculcates the belief in a visible return of Christ, or the practice of feet-washing, or the sacrament of triple immersion, or the obligation to treat disease without medicine, these sects multiply their converts. The reason why so many literalists are not enrolled in the churches is not because they do not sufficiently accept the authority of the Bible, but because, through the multiplicity of disagreeing interpreters, they are confused in their minds as to what the Bible really does definitely teach. Some man — or woman — with vigorous, domineering personality, who can make his interpretations of Scripture more definite to the popular mind than rival sectarian leaders, is the chief explanation of every one of several remarkable cults that have spread] in America. In contrast to the literalists are the idealists, as those may be termed who assume that religion is not the product of a book, but that the Book is a product of religion. They believe that religion is not obedience to a recorded law, but a life whose motive power is the Infinite Spirit. They accept the Bible not as the source of that life but as a means for its development. To them interpretations of the Bible are of great but not of supreme importance. Over these idealists, using the term in this very limited and inaccurate sense, no sect based merely on an explanation of Scripture text can have much if any influence. The literalists in America to-day are quite as dependent upon the letter as literalists always have been. The idealists, however, are much more in accord with modern intellectual tendencies, and, though probably very much in the minority, are, in my opinion, decidedly growing in numbers and influence. This is particularly true of clergymen.

Is there any likelihood that the experience of this country will be like that of France, where, as is commonly supposed, there is a definite line of demarcation between the few devoted adherents of the Church, composed chiefly of clerics and women, and the great body of the population, which is indifferent to the Church, except as an institution for the performance of certain formalities? Decidedly and emphatically, no. For three reasons. To paraphrase the saying of Demosthenes, the first is liberty, the second is liberty, and the third is liberty.

In the first place, the religious impulse in America, quite otherwise than in France, has been left free from political interference. In France, as indeed in a large part of Europe, a man's attitude toward the Church is determined, not only by religious faith, but also by political considerations. In the United States, a man in determining his attitude toward the Church is free to be governed solely by religious motive. That there is a difference in effect from this difference of condition is obvious.

In the second place, religion in America has been allowed to meet knowledge freely, on an open field. In France religion is confined, on the one hand, to the ignorant and superstitious who are not bothered with intellectual difficulties, and, on the other hand, the highly educated few who have the trained vision to see that religion is not identical with its traditional forms. The great bulk of the people who have knowledge enough to see that traditional forms of religion are incompatible with reality, and yet who have not knowledge enough to see that these traditional forms are not identical with religion, are, for the most part, those who are alienated. In America the very weakness of Christianity — namely, its multiple forms — is its strength; for it is constant evidence that these forms cannot be religion. Religion in America is probably vaguer, but it is not impossible to the ordinary intelligence, as it is in France. The recent religious movements among students in American colleges offer a concrete illustration of the effect that intellectual liberty has had in preserving religious vitality in America.

In the third place, the people of America are intellectually and morally free to follow the guidance of intellectual and moral leaders. It has been shown that in America it takes about a generation for a new idea, well established by experts, to become popularly disseminated and accepted. It has been true in politics, in education, in religion, more than once. A professor of Church history once was asked by a student whether a statement regarding the early Church made by a professor of philosophy was sound. " No," was the answer; " that was the hypothesis thirty years ago, but a different conclusion has since been definitely established. Church history is not his department, so he is about thirty years behind the Church historians. I suppose I am about thirty years behind the metaphysicians." Each of those professors represented in turn the people, while the other represented the leader. If, therefore, the present position of leaders in religious thought can be accepted as a guide, future religious life in America will be marked by tendencies toward a religion less dependent upon intellectual hypotheses, and therefore less timid of intellectual change; toward a faith less dependent upon the external bulwark of literalism; toward a less materialistic interpretation of life; toward a religion more ethical in character; toward a desire for beauty of religious expression, at any rate in public worship; toward a more confident belief in the reality of religious experience; and toward a more frequent recourse to the Christian Church in its various forms and through its various instrumentalities, not so much for doctrine as for the expression of devotional feeling, for ethical impulse, and for opportunities of doing good after the teaching and practice of Jesus of Nazareth.